Tomorrow's News

ALSO BY R. L. DUFFUS

Williamstown Branch
The Waterbury Record
The Tower of Jewels
Nostalgia, USA
Adventure in Retirement
Queen Calafia's Island
Jimmy's Place

Tomorrow's News

A Primer for Prophets

By R. L. Duffus

···

W · W · NORTON & COMPANY · INC ·

New York

Contents

Processional   7

I.   Too Many People?   *11*

II.   Where Is Everybody?   *29*

III.   Preparing: for What?   *40*

IV.   The International Fire Department   *49*

V.   The Happy Isles   *69*

VI.   Motion: The Modern Neurosis   *81*

VII.   Moon Madness   *101*

VIII.   Army of the Potomac   *115*

IX.   Big Business, Big Labor   *126*

X.   By the Sweat of our Brows   *138*

XI.   The Job of Being Free   *150*

Recessional   *159*

Processional

A NUMBER of circumstances in recent years have made many of us wonder whether man is a permanent fixture on this earth, and also whether he ought to be.

Contrasted with what seem to us the lower forms of life, man has had magnificent opportunities. He has used some of them magnificently, others meanly. What does it signify, now, when the highest form of intelligence we know of in the universe (and we can't be too sure of that) is unable to secure its own survival? Or when it begins to play so many tricks with the earth that the earth's own Creator might not recognize His handiwork?

I raise these questions because some of the wicked, foolish, and unfortunate things the human race is doing make such doubts seem appropriate. The problem is made more difficult by the very splendor of some human achievements.

I wish to make it plain that I am not plotting to overthrow the human race by force and violence. Nor do I have any precise remedies for what is wrong with us. I do not believe in pre-cooked, deep-frozen, ready-to-use systems of any sort.

The trouble with us is that though we have our concepts of greatness, goodness, and beauty, we don't consistently live up to them. We have consciences, which I doubt any other animal has. We can be ashamed of ourselves—a feat of which no other creature that we know is capable.

The present handbook is not a learned tome. For one thing, it is not heavy enough to be a tome and the learning is what all of us who can read and do elementary worrying can pick up in the course of a fairly long life. There are some problems today that all of us have to face. The experts, specialists, and other learned men do what they can to enlighten us about them; but in many instances I suspect that we will have to act or counteract now and read the books afterward. The common sense we all hope we have will not build a computer or improve the quality of corn, but if we grasp a few fundamentals, it may help save us from collective suicide.

So what I propose to do is to consider some of our human dilemmas as they occur to me, and try to guess how serious they are and what to do about them.

I have arranged my topics in the order that seemed most important. The first two chapters are devoted to the basic questions of how the human race can keep from becoming too numerous or not numerous enough. If we are not going to do either of these things we had better get some ant to write books like this.

Tomorrow's News

I

....

Too Many People?

EVERY ADULT person with even a limited experience in life and a smattering of modern fiction knows what causes babies. Many of them now know what prevents babies. Hence I feel no need to enlarge upon this subject, except to suggest that prevention is better than cure.

The trouble is that too many babies are being produced. World population is growing at the rate of about 2 percent annually—compounded every day.

None of us can logically object to babies, for we once were such—and in most cases our friends and relatives said we were cute. I saw some brand-new infants the other day, behind glass in a hospital, with the proud fathers doing everything except turn handsprings outside. I should judge that these babies are healthier than those that used to be born in log cabins and other picturesque but unsanitary places. They will be better cared for than babies used to be, during infancy, childhood, and maturity, and unless something pretty awful happens, will live longer than human beings used to do.

But babies take room. And as they grow older they demand more room. If we eventually produce more babies than the earth can support, we can blame it on Nature, if that makes us feel better. I use the word "Nature" to suggest a composite of forces—not a female that we can complain about to the celestial Police; it is a convenient word.

In creating and controlling all living things Nature made what today can only be regarded as a mistake: she worked on a theory of scarcity and took it for granted that the only way to get enough of any living thing is to get too much of it. Millions of sperm cells may be expended to impregnate a single animal or insect female; millions may be squandered by a beetle to keep the tribe of beetles going; the elephant is a thoughtful animal with a long period of gestation, but if it were not for various restrictive factors, the whole earth in a few generations would be completely blanketed with elephants. And so on with all the other species, including our own.

Nature installed in every living thing the instinct and the apparatus to multiply. Then she made them compete against each other. Man's wars, terrible though they have been, are trivial compared with the eternal, built-in wars that pervade creation. If an organism becomes too abundant some other organism will cut off its food, or, quite simply, eat *it*. One insect eats another; one animal eats another; one flower, tree, or shrub crowds out another—and sometimes, as in the case of parasitic growths, consumes it. A number of blights devour growing plants and trees—the elm, the potato, corn, cotton. These vegetable assassins have no malice—they are merely trying to earn an honest living. Nature arranged all this, on one of her numerous off-days. I do not think it was bright of Nature to do this. I do not think it was kind.

But I think of those babies in the hospital, behind the protecting glass. They are a part of the worldwide population explosion. Which ones would the dourest population specialist say are unnecessary?

2.

I am not sure that Nature intended to make man the overpowering creature he has become. Evidently she first conceived of him, however, as something that needed coddling. There were so many other creatures willing and eager to bite him; some of them weighed much more than he did. Nature therefore gave him powers of reproduction far beyond his later and present needs. Then she went away on another job.

Man in his early days really did lead an exciting life. Indeed, to an impartial observer, it would have seemed as though his chances of survival were slim. Nature made quite a few experiments that failed; man might have been one of them.

At the beginning he was a hunter, not a rancher, and therefore had to depend on what he could catch or find. He may have eaten chiefly wild plants, berries, and roots before he attempted to kill living game. Circumstances beyond his control sometimes removed the animals and plants on which he depended for food.

Primitive man fished, which is of course a form of hunting. He did not go to the Banks of Newfoundland, however. Until he invented boats—and when he did that he was not primitive any more—he could not yet go into deep water. He could gather shellfish, and on many shores, from the London River to the coast of California, he did this. But a disease might temporarily remove the shellfish, and so leave him hungry. He could eat seaweed, but a blight could kill the seaweed for a time. He was dependent on Mother Nature, and Mother Nature often let him down. Maybe she wanted to make him self-reliant. More likely, she was merely busy at something else—perfecting poison ivy, for example.

Man had enemies, too. Or should we say enemies, when all they wanted was something to eat? Man was attacked and devoured by wild animals of various sorts. He was bitten by poisonous snakes who resented his intrusion on their privacy. He had diseases, just as we do today, only more of them; he usually attributed these to evil spirits, and his methods of driving out evil spirits were not what we would call scientific medicine today. He was plagued by changes in the climate. His life was, as Hobbes said, nasty, brutish, and short. He was not a noble savage but a member of the lower classes in the animal kingdom.

But Nature continued, in her well-established way, to keep the human race prolific. Since woman's life was short she had a brief production period, but she worked hard at it. She was probably almost constantly pregnant. Large families must have been the rule in most primitive societies; it may have taken one child a year to keep them so.

For most of the children died, as Nature assumed they would. Only the tough and lucky ones survived; Nature evidently thought that this was good for an evolving race. The human birth rate during the long prehistoric ages before 6000 B.C. has been estimated at 50 percent—or about twice the figure reached by this generation in the United

States. The population grew, but not rapidly.

So far Nature had planned with seeming wisdom: the human race was staying on earth and was growing slowly in numbers, but men weren't taking the whole tract over, or stepping on one another's toes. There was plenty of room.

In 6000 B.C., the students of the subject estimate, there may have been five million people on the globe—about two-thirds the present population of New York City or half the present population of Tokyo. By the beginning of the Christian era possibly three hundred million people or perhaps only two hundred million, according to which computer is doing the guessing, were in existence. There could be no world census. How many were in China, Japan, India? Nobody knows.

By 1650 A.D. the world total may have risen to five hundred million. Now it is in the neighborhood of three billion, and growing at the rate of fifty million (about the population of France) each year. So one begins to wonder if Nature has not over-reached herself.

3.

Such a question may not mean much, for we do not know what Nature intended to accomplish, or whether she had any intentions at all. All we can be sure of is that Nature does manage to accumulate vast numbers of creatures in our own and other species, and that if these become too numerous she provides a remedy in the form of famine, disease, climatic change, or the efforts of competing forms of life. Humanity has increased slowly over the ages because the sperm cells, the ova, and the babies, though produced in incredible quantities, were for the most part thrown away.

We might better grasp the workings of this process if we were to imagine the Detroit motor car manufacturers making seven or eight million vehicles a year, and then sending a hundred thousand into the market and scrapping the others. This, I suppose, would not be considered good business, but it would keep the motor car alive as a species.

At any rate, during most of its history humanity has operated on this principle. It has had an extremely narrow profit margin. Women had to go through childbirth without much help from Nature or the doctors. Midwives probably helped a little, from the earliest times. But it was a man's world—not a mother's or baby's world. In some African tribes women ranked just below the cattle.

Certain factors restricted population in rude ways. One was the custom of exposing or drowning girl babies, who obviously couldn't breed if they didn't survive. In some primitive societies a man might have many wives. In such societies many men had to remain womanless, for the oldest profession had not been invented. A side effect may have been a curtailing of births.

The Black Death was not the only destructive disease. Nature seemed to be as much concerned with various microorganisms, such as those causing scarlet fever, diphtheria, typhoid, tetanus, sleeping sickness, tuberculosis, and leprosy, as she was with human beings. She may have toyed with the thought of making one of these the dominant species on earth.

She played no favorites: the lion and the leopard were

dear to her, the malarial mosquito and the plague-bearing flea; the poisonous spider and the bedbug; all, under Nature's impartial plan, had a fair chance to survive and multiply.

To a human being it does not seem terrible that the sperm of the solitary bee, the Surinam toad, the whale, or the hippopotamus should be wasted by premature death or failure to live at all.

It does seem terrible to a human being, however, that so many potential human creatures, so many millions somewhat like himself, should have been so briefly touched with the finger of existence. What poets, musicians, scientists, statesmen and plain good old Joes there may have been among them!

Good or bad, however, this is Nature's way. She sows a million seeds where only a small patch of crop could grow; she throws away enough animals, plants, birds, and men to populate a million reservations.

But this practice of creating only to abandon ceased in man's case as soon as he began to influence his own fate. He became more and more resistant to famine, cold, heat, and disease—in short, harder to kill. But Nature, possibly a little bewildered, never having encountered anything like this before, continued to make too many human beings. This is now our problem and maybe Nature's, too.

It is clear that man must have seemed to Nature a more promising experiment than the pterodactyl and the icthyosaurus; these were mechanically defective and out of drawing. Man was not only a convenient size; he also began to master his environment. No other living creature had done that; no other had looked backward and forward, recognized its own mistakes, and arranged to do it better next time.

Up to the time of man, Nature's way of improving living conditions for a species was to give free rein to what might be called the dying conditions. The weak and bungling, the animals that were too heavy for light work or too light for heavy work perished; this taught them a lesson, and it was the only way Nature could think of to instruct them; they died as individuals and often as a species and were not in a position to complain.

But when man blundered he did not necessarily die; he merely tried a new and better way. He developed an attribute we call intelligence. I do not know what this is, but it enables a person or a race to make continuing experiments and to profit by the results. A species of birds dies out if its eggs don't hatch. Man, on the other hand, invents the incubator. Man counts on his fingers or toes and comes up with the decimal system; this is the beginning of mathematics, and after a while we have computers.

A flock of bees can make a better hive than a human being could, but no bee can explain why or how. I have yet to come on a book about honey written by a bee.

To add up: Nature continues to treat us as though we were in danger of extinction—we aren't. Nature makes us just as fertile as were our ancestors during the ice ages, which we no longer need to be. Her plan to keep us alive but scared has gone sour. We know a lot about how to stay alive now. We are not so scared. The result is overproduction.

4.

When I was a junior in college the population experts had an enchanting theory: large families were the result of poverty and ignorance. What else could the poor do with so little expense? But if we raised the level of well-being, the rate of population increase would drop and the danger of over-population (especially of the wrong people) would diminish. What man and woman would bother to have more than 2.4 children if they could afford to go to the movies or buy an automobile instead?

The theory seemed to be justified by what the comfortable economic middle classes actually did. They bred discretely. Two children would replace the parents; the extra, purely statistical four-tenths of a child was to compensate for early deaths, failures to mate, or sterile unions.

Some sociologists were startled by the figure. They said that the well-to-do—who, after all, paid the salaries—were demonstrably more intelligent and of better stock than the poor, and that the unfortunate tendency of the poor to have too many children would lower the quality of the race. This was an appalling doctrine, for the ability to make money is not of necessity linked with other worthy qualities. The investigators had merely discovered that the better-educated were the better-educated; what seemed like superior intelligence was often nothing more than the result of having nothing to worry about, plus enough to eat.

Then the middle classes began to breed. Instead of an average of two and four-tenths of a child per family, they tended to have four, five, even six children. There was an upsurge after the First World War, likewise after the Second. As late as the mid-1950's some students of population were predicting that the United States would level off at a maximum between 175 million and 200 million. As I write, the actual figure is approaching 200 million, although the rate of increase has fallen somewhat.

But we continue to multiply. Something similar has occurred all over the earth. The less developed countries of Asia, Africa, and South America have not bred any faster than they always did, but their people now die less frequently of unnecessary or curable diseases.

The increase is about 2 percent for the tabulated portions of mankind; it ranges from nearly that much in North America to nearly 3 percent in Central America. That is, almost all of us are becoming more numerous, but some of us are becoming more numerous more rapidly than others. The earth's power balances are changing at the same time that the population trends are growing more alarming.

A few elderly persons remember when the Western Allies, including those sterling defenders of human liberties, the Kaiser's Germany and feudal Japan, as well as the United States and Britain, marched to Peking to relieve their besieged legations, put down the Boxer Rebellion, and incidentally to pick up a little gravy for themselves. This was at the turn of the present century. We do not do this sort of thing any more, although mainland China is far less free than Germany and Japan were then. We do not think it right any more; nor is it possible. Nor do we explore darkest Africa and appropriate its choicest areas for white exploitation or control. On the contrary, we permit African tribes or nations to set up shop for themselves. At the moment South Africa and Rhodesia are resisting this trend, but one guesses they will not hold out permanently. Despite much disorder, the peoples of the newly liberated lands wax and increase, in numbers and in power.

All this is discouraging to the white man, to the extent that he yearns to continue his ancient mastery of other people's lands. It is encouraging for the man with a black, yellow, or bronze skin, who never did like being kicked around by strangers and now doesn't usually have to be.

The situation would be more promising for the human race as a whole if it produced a feeling of brotherhood, regardless of color or of the shapes of noses, lips, and heads, but this has not yet occurred. And the white man, being in a minority, has to watch his step in this swiftly changing world. Otherwise he may regret it.

Estimates of future world population run into incredible billions. The impending danger, however, is not that the earth will become so crowded that each person will be fortunate if he finds room enough to lie down. The danger resides in the more immediate troubles sure to be caused—indeed, already stirred up—by the inequality of land and income among nations and races, civilizations and continents.

The bearded revolutionist who spent so much time a century and more ago reading in the British Museum in London and committing his Teutonic dogma to a book he called *Das Kapital* was dead wrong about the class war. The poor have not been growing poorer, though some of them have grown rich.

The existing inequality is of a different sort than Marx foresaw and is not likely to be cured by formulas. A worldwide communism might turn humanity into one vast subsistence anthill, but humanity on the whole doesn't seem to care that much for ants.

5.

The rigors of an unequally dense and unequally increasing population in different countries do not threaten us with revolution; they threaten us with international war. And we have now reached a technological stage where even a victory in a good-sized international war is like a doctor curing his patient by cutting his head off.

In figures and percentages, the human situation is terrifying. Not so long ago North America was said by geographers to have 16 percent of the earth's area, 9 percent of its population, and 43 percent of its income. Average family income in North America, $1,000. Average family income in East Asia, $50.

A further sinister fact is that although the underdeveloped countries have been making progress, the more fortunate lands have made more; the gap between the two is widening, not narrowing.

The poorer people in the United States—the inhabitants of distress areas, urban or rural—have much to complain about. They may have television sets—who hasn't? But they cannot dress well. They often have automobiles—how can a man go to work these days, or to market, or to church, without one?—but these are old and dilapidated. They have better medical care than their parents had, but in the rural areas good doctors and hospitals are far from plentiful. Their children do not have favorable opportunities for higher education or for advancement in life.

Yet anybody now living in the economic bottom strattum of the United States is rich contrasted with a person of the lowest economic stratum in India, Ghana, or Brazil. Not only does he have a heritage of freedom, but he also has an assurance of at least enough food to keep him alive and at least sufficient shelter to keep him out of bad weather.

We have snobs but not castes. We do not have famine; indeed, one of them major headaches of our time in the United States is what to do with an over-abundance of food, and how much to pay the farmer for not producing.

We live within our fenced acreage, two persons to a unit of space, which in China's mainland, under whatever form of government, must accommodate seven. How can we justify this and what ought we to do about it? Will the rest of the world indefinitely put up with it? What will we do if we are required to move over?

These questions do enter into any view of mankind's future. I think the mainland Chinese—the people, not the peculiar government—or the inhabitants of the Indian peninsula (famine-stricken in early 1966) have a grievance. They may contend that we in our own country have latched on to more than our share of the earth. We may reply, in Voltaire's words, let them cultivate their own gardens; but I would take care to be ready to run if I were about to say this to a desperately hungry man.

On the other hand, I don't believe the terrestrial level of happiness would be any higher if our frontiers, like those of Oklahoma in the land rush days, were freely open to the first comers; I do not think turning the Mississippi Valley into a Yangtze Basin or an Indus watershed would do any lasting good.

Unlimited immigration has in fact been tried, all through human history—and probably earlier. The strong tribes have moved whenever the grazing grew poor. Or when stronger tribes pushed them, usually, for some profound reason, toward the West.

The anthropologists say that today's Europe is a melting pot of at least three types of humanity. Even the Swiss are so mixed up that they have to communicate in four languages. The ancient Roman Empire began to be born when the Romans pushed north into the territory of the Etruscans. The Romans themselves were a mixed stock, with some African intermixture in the South. Malta is a bouillabaisse of many ingredients. Sicily has taken in ancient Romans, Greeks, Scandinavians, and North Africans.

What is France? A mélange of diverse races that in medieval times did not even have a common language. Whence does the word Normandy derive? There are racial remnants all over Europe, but especially in the West—the Basques, the Bretons; in Britain the Cornish, the Welsh and the Highland Scots; in Ireland another assortment of Celts, re-learning in modern times a language they had almost forgotten. The English themselves are Angles, Saxons, Jutes, Normans, with a sprinkling of Italians, French, Germans, Jews, and others.

Let us consider our own country. Our nearly two hundred million have largely dispossessed, segregated, or absorbed a million Indians, who were themselves a hodgepodge of races and languages, frequently fighting among themselves for desirable hunting grounds.

Take Central and South America, or if you like, Africa south of the Sahara. In each case migrations changed the face of the country and of history. In Brazil the Portuguese took over long ago and introduced Negro slavery. Now the Negroes in Brazil are as free as anybody. There is less discrimination against them than you would find in New York City or Los Angeles. Spaniards and Italians flowed into Venezuela and also into the Argentine, Peru, and other Latin American lands.

These mixtures show that even in modern times people could and did migrate. The figures do not show, of course, that migration can today be a cure of over-population. It may sometimes seem a cure, as it did in the United States during the nineteenth century. There was the free land; there were the surplus families to move in on it. These migrations meant taking land away from those who owned it—usually the Indians, but in one case the Government and citizens of Mexico. This continent was thus conquered by brave men and by noble, tough-fibered women, but the plan was the ancient one that those shall take who have the power and those may keep who can.

I am glad that the North European races (and some from Southern Europe) got control of what is now the United States, and that the land and riches were not left to the native Indians or—worse yet—conquered by the Aztecs. The outcome was, as it used to be called, manifest destiny, but ethical it was not. I glory in it, as I was brought up to do. I just wonder sometimes. Anyhow, it can't happen again, here or anywhere else.

6.

A nightmare comes and sits on me sometimes in the middle of the night. It is this: suppose we in the United States found ourselves subject to colonization as the Oriental and

African objects of Western solicitude once did. Suppose the white man, as one of what Kipling called the lesser breeds, became the yellow man's or the black man's burden. What then?

We more or less white men took control of the Far East and of nearly all the non-white world for a period of three or four hundred years. We had quite a run for our money. Now, suppose the Orient and other now underdeveloped countries and lands decide not only to run their own show, as they are mostly doing at the moment, but to colonize the Occident; suppose some excess of population, backed by some quirk of invention, enables them to do this.

Shudderingly I think of Chinese gunboats or their modernized equivalent keeping order up and down the Mississippi, Missouri, Hudson, Sacramento, Columbia, and Winooski rivers. My horrified eyes try to visualize Boston, New York, Baltimore, New Orleans, San Francisco, Los Angeles, Portland, Seattle, and the Great Lakes cities as treaty ports. I am driven to imagine a war between China and India as to which one shall have a sphere of influence in Rhode Island. I picture Indonesia lapping up, one by one, the islands of the Caribbean. I see Buddhism, Taoism, Confucianism, and Mohammedanism coming, not as fascinating exotic religions, but with fleets and guns behind them, to replace Christianity.

But these activities would settle no problem, not even the problem of population. Look at China, the most populous of our potential adversaries. I may mention three figures. One is the present population of China, which may well be in the neighborhood of seven hundred million. A second figure is the population of the United States—as we have seen, about two hundred million. A third is the estimated annual increase in the entire world's population—about fifty million. In fourteen or fifteen years the aggregate of this increase would be about equal to the present population of China. This means that migration, either in armed hordes or through Ellis Island, is no permanent cure for too many people.

Our former wards, and as we used to say, dependents, may be all dressed up but they really have no place to go. There can be no successful attempt by any race or nation to out-multiply any other race or nation. That way is a street marked No Thoroughfare. Preponderant populations may represent an excess of power—but the power will have its limits. No world empire will again be possible, no Roman, British, Chinese, Russian, or American dominion. No salesman will be able to sell the line. The results could not be made to seem worth the trouble.

Genghis Khan, Attila, Charlemagne, Napoleon, Hitler, Stalin—all are equally out of date; their bones, their maniacal aspirations, their whole array of tawdry goods, these are in the dust. Today they seem silly, wicked, and pitiful.

In the swift multiplication of our species, made possible by Nature's inelasticity and our own manifold inventions, we have a problem that has gone beyond politics and creeds, beyond systems, beyond the wildest dreams of ambitious fools.

How are we going to stop producing more people than the earth can comfortably carry? This is the formidable question of the age. No more can there be the march of multitudes, pressing into green and untouched lands or driving out the aborigines to provide farms for their self-styled superiors.

Let today's trends continue for another quarter of a century, with population outrunning food, as it now does, and there will be sure disaster. Whether or not it will continue is even more important than who wins the next World Series, I should think.

Killing babies is not a remedy. Abortion is cruel and dangerous. A harmless pill, intelligently used, will probably do what is needed. This is one of the things that ought to be written into the future.

The problem of some races or nations increasing more rapidly than others will still remain. If this is not solved on a worldwide basis it will not be solved at all. The H-bomb, which I would like to consider next, might solve it temporarily—but not in a nice way.

II

⚹⚹⚹⚹⚹⚹⚹

Where Is Everybody?

THE TAG END of a once chronic anecdote about the H-bomb is the remark, "Where is everybody?" This is a pertinent inquiry, for there is a doubt as to where everybody's mind, knowledge, and soul were when the H-bomb (or its puny sister, the A-bomb) was invented and let loose. We all know that by two gigantic strokes the A-bomb helped win a war, although the people killed were largely innocent civilians, and the war was perhaps already won when the bomb came on the stage.

Most of us assume that nothing would have more delighted the late Adolf Hitler than to be able to lay low Paris, London, Rome, Moscow, Washington, and New York, from his Berlin bunker, by pressing half a dozen buttons.

The bomb, it has been explained, was cheap for what it did. It was no more cruel than the spear, the arrow, the old-fashioned musket ball, the poetic sword that sliced live men like so much beef, or the napalm (jellied petroleum) bombs that set human beings as well as structures on fire; we were already using napalm over Germany and Japan when we dropped the quick and almost painless atomic explosives on the two Japanese cities.

Two facts may be noted about the atomic bomb: first, it was a logical product of the industrial revolution—a labor-saving device; second, it was, like most modern industry, impersonal and manufactured for a wide variety of clients. Babies were killed in Hiroshima and Nagasaki, but they were never seen by the wholesome American boys who killed them.

And indeed the trouble with the atomic bomb is not its savagery. The trouble is its efficiency. This efficiency, in some form, might have been foreseen by almost anyone familiar with the history of the industrial arts. Some scientists, and even some military brass hats, did foresee it. Gifted minds in the Allied countries and in Germany were struck almost simultaneously with the happy perception: how convenient it would be if one airplane with one explosive could be made to do the work of a thousand airplanes with a thousand bombs.

The Atomic Energy Commission has not taken me into its confidence, but I am sure that one plane with one bomb can do far more today than even ten thousand planes with conventional bombs (and how sweetly Victorian that sounds!) could formerly manage.

2.

A long time ago I wrote a magazine article in which I argued that the nineteenth century assumption of continuous and almost effortless progress had been destroyed by the First World War. I still believe this was a respectable minor prophecy, borne out by subsequent events, including the Second World War and its aftermath. Evolution, as many people now sadly realize, doesn't necessarily mean movement toward the higher and nobler elements of human (or other) life. We might evolve downhill, as Hitler's Germany certainly did.

A great many persons still alive must recall the emotional shock of our first two A-bombs dropped in war. Few felt like cheering when the news came through. Many must have wondered, as I did, whether this was prelude or finish. In a way, it was both. Japan quickly surrendered. At this writing the bomb has not been used again in war—the old one or the shiny new ones now in hand. Not yet. Maybe never. One has to put in the qualifying word. That is the difference between the pre-bomb world and the post-bomb world. There has been no certainty on this point since August, 1945.

Nor will there ever be any certainty as long as the life of man endures. The bomb is a permanent fact. Neither a dictatorship of the right nor a tyranny of the left nor a complete and blessed democracy can kill the atomic weapon; not one of these can do more than chain it to its kennel. The moving finger has written.

We are caught in our own trap. We can by international agreement abolish the existing stock of atomic weapons, though as yet the nations do not trust one another enough for that. But we cannot abolish the knowledge mankind now has as to how to make and convey an atomic bomb.

Nor can we separate the lethal portions of our atomic lore from the useful and wholesome ones; for if you can cure cancer, run a power plant, take the salt out of water, or modify the genes in an unborn living organism by the use of atomic energy, you can't forget how to eliminate New York City or Peking with it. The shadow still hangs over us, and always will.

It is a peculiar shadow, because most persons ignore it as much as they can. From time to time we are given carefully veiled indications of what the new H-bombs are like and can do. The authorities dare not tell us everything, since to do so (as they point out) would tell our potential enemies everything, too; so, in the matter of information in this field, we are classified with Moscow and Peking. As a democratic society we lay down principles and elect or accept leaders to carry them out. Then we are told to run along and play and not ask foolish questions. And then the authorities worry because we are not as scared as they think we ought to be.

The truth is that some things are too awful to believe, like the old-fashioned Calvinistic notion of hell. I cannot believe that the later versions of the H-bomb will do what it is whispered they will do—the effort strains my imagination and makes my head ache. I cannot believe that a people still subscribing to Lincoln's Gettysburg Address are doing such things, and consider it essential and good to do them. I try, and fail. The necessity may be apparent; the reality is not. I am not criticizing my country or its people. It is an entire generation of the human race, all of us everywhere without exception, that is at fault or in error, in not inventing a new morality to match the new technology.

The new generation may find a way out, and one less silly than demonstrations and protest marches. For ours is an age of great vitality, not of moody helplessness and hopelessness. The beatnick is even now an outworn symbol. Today's young people are not half so forlorn as the so-called "lost generation" after the First World War. We may be declining and falling, but nobody, old or young, seems to believe it. If they did they would be like the Millerites of the early nineteenth century, who were so sure the world was coming to an end on a certain day that they made a sort of fire sale of their possessions, put on sheets as ascension robes and went up on a hill one fine morning to wait.

We ought to be very sad. The same science that conferred the bomb on us is quite capable of producing new gases that will lay whole cities low without permanently injuring the buildings. This would be handy for an aggressor; he could simply remove the corpses, disinfect and dust the furniture, purify the water system, move in and live happily ever after—or until some envious neighbor, with a different gas, aggressed against him.

Or perhaps, as has been ingeniously suggested, the attacking force could introduce an artificial new disease, first inoculating its own personnel against contamination.

Science, indeed, awaits our bidding. Like Nature, it is eager to experiment. The men who practice it are no better and no worse than the rest of us. Mostly they are more curious, more painstaking, and in their way, more intelligent. They long to find out what will happen if you introduce ingredient x into the existing mixture abc. The earth may wither like a lawn in a dry August or bloom like a rose in June under their ministrations, or even disappear entirely; the scientists will want to know why.

3.

Some of what I have just been writing sounds anti-science, even to me. I do not mean to give this impression. To kill or suppress science would be not only impracticable but immoral. What I am suggesting, out of the depths of my laymanship, is that the scientists become more scientific; that they consider the total effects on human life of their devices, inventions, and discoveries, not merely the impact in a single narrow sector, that when they think up ingenious ways in which to kill us, they also try to contrive new ways to keep us alive and make us happier and more productive. The specialization of some scientists in killing us and of other scientists in curing us is deadly; the boys ought to get together in this matter.

We cannot keep the human race from trying to find things out. We are irresistibly drawn to new inventions, and adventurous caprices and ideas; these are our intellectual catnip. This is why we are down on the ground walking, or driving motor vehicles, or being rushed through the air (often with motion pictures to keep us from being bored) at speeds much faster than sound. Nature made us so. We had better stay so.

Nature may have assumed that we would do ourselves more good than harm with this strange instinct, and in spite of all evidence to the contrary, I am inclined to believe we have and shall. We all have at times at least a small share of the scientific drive; hence the crowds that watch excavation and new construction in cities or gather avidly at the scenes of accidents and crimes.

A person with the true scientific instinct can not only

take a clock apart but can even put it together again and make it run better than ever. He can change his own typewriter ribbon without even soiling his fingers. He can use atomic energy for good purposes, if opportunity offers, as well as for bad ones. I am not a scientist, because I cannot do these things; I respect those who can.

I have talked with physicists who were sad and sorry when the first large-scale atomic experiment at Alamogordo actually worked; they had hoped it wouldn't. The best of them—and they are pretty good—are, I am sure, afflicted like the rest of us by the whole lethal business. They may have a lurking curiosity as to how the moon would look if blasted in two by a super-duper, economy-size H-bomb, and what the effect would be on the tides and young love; they may even wonder if after a while the march of enlightenment may not enable them to disintegrate the earth itself.

As a rule, however, I imagine that most of the H-bomb experts realize they have a bear by the tail and would like to let go; they are husbands and fathers, they garden or play golf, their wives go to bridge parties, they want to send their children to college, they would not care to have their routine interrupted by a too prodigious success. They are good people. They may even, like Professor Einstein, play the violin fairly well. Professionally, they appear to take an almost pathetic interest in helping people stay alive rather than in exterminating them.

There is, for instance, the plan to take the salt out of sea water by the use of nuclear energy; this is in line with an act passed by Congress in 1952. Conferences of international agencies on Peaceful Uses of Atomic Energy have been held in Geneva. The United States has even talked these matters over with the Soviet Government.

We really don't want to destroy one another. We would prefer to use nuclear power to give one another a drink, cure or prevent disease, improve the growth of plants and the breed of horses, add to our store of useful knowledge. Today's experiments with nuclear energy for peaceful purposes are glittering. Enough de-salted water, introduced on the California coast somewhere between Los Angeles and San Diego, might transform the Mojave and Colorado deserts into living spaces for millions. The Great Salt Lake might be tapped and purified.

If the applied energy of the atom can water a lawn in Redlands or Hartford, or run a cooling system in Tucson, maybe we can get our minds off what it can do to lay mighty cities desolate.

4.

I believe, however, we laymen will have to look at science with more information and less reverence. A scientist is not a magician or a superman. He is something far more formidable, an ordinary man using extraordinary tools. He is apt to be above the average in intelligence but he is not necessarily an intellectual giant with his head in the clouds. But he shares a common heritage with the rest of us. Shakespeare may emerge without warning from a society hardly out of barbarism, but Einstein needed a long procession of gifted men behind him, including Aristotle, Archimedes, Leonardo, and Newton.

Such geniuses are scarcely numerous, but they are the real aristocracy of the human race. Have we not all speculated on how spacious a room we would need to contain all the real makers and masters of our culture from the dawn of history to the present day? I suppose a telephone booth would be too small, but Grand Central Station or the Hollywood Bowl would be far too big.

Such speculations do not get us anywhere; they are like a child's dream as he lies in the warm grass, listening to the hum of insects on an August day. No magic figures summoned from the vast deep can change civilization all by themselves. The wheel, the alphabet, the now almost obsolete steam engine, the heavier-than-air flying machine, the wireless transmission of sound, images, and color all had first to be conceived, no doubt, by individuals, but they had to be developed by teams and groups; all these inventions and many more. Seldom have the basic knowledge and the methods of use been lost. Even though we have forgotten how to make stained glass as beautiful as that of the Cathedral of Chartres, we are still not likely to forget how to make skyscrapers, suspension bridges, Scotch whisky, rubber, a wide variety of synthetics and steel. A man of normal intelligence can go to school and learn how to make such things or some small part of them—or more remarkable yet, to show others how to make them.

Man's invention of ways to produce and control fire was a Promethean gesture that traditionally trespassed on the premises of the gods. From the first man-made fire to the explosion of the first nuclear bomb at Alamogordo the line is direct, undeviating, and inevitable.

Meanwhile, all through the ages, man has been adjusting his environment to his desires and needs. The hunters and farmers of olden days began to go into cities; the cities, in

ancient, medieval, and early modern times, consisted
largely of what today we should regard as slums, with a
few public buildings set magnificently among them. Today
a modern city is far healthier than an old-style backwoods
farm. Urban or rural, we began to control our environment, making a better job of it in many cases than Nature
ever did.

In brief, the human race is now in a position to do about
what it wants to do with itself and with the world. That is,
I think, what the bomb means. That is the realization of the
Promethean ideal.

5.

We control all forms of life, our own included. We can
abolish any kind of life if we feel like it—though we may
have some trouble with a number of insect breeds. We may
be able to influence genetics in various ways; we may be
able to turn out human beings as well as other animals in
any pattern desired, possibly without the aid of a male-
parent.

This thought gives me the creeps. Who is going to decide
what sort of human beings it is best to have? A dictator
might prefer individuals who would work hard and not
talk back. Or he might like a variety: strong ones for heavy
lifting and the secret police; patient ones for machine tend-
ing; ornamental ones for television and motion pictures;
flexible ones to do the propaganda; funny ones for court
fools; killers for getting rid of human experiments that
didn't fit into the dictatorial society—poets, philosophers,
thinkers, rebels, and such misfits.

I don't put it beyond well-meaning and inquisitive minds

among us to work toward this project—not trying to decide whether it would be a good thing, but curious as to whether it could be done at all. Creation is quite a responsibility, but if we can achieve the controlled production of life—and I don't mean by the old-fashioned way—I'm afraid we'll try.

Nuclear energy, in its menace and its promise, is a symbol of many surprising things mankind can achieve. This is a truth by which we can steady ourselves in these strange, swiftly moving times. It deepens, for good or evil, the meaning of all we do. It imposes on the human race an overwhelming responsibility. There may be other intelligent beings in the universe, as Walter Sullivan points out in *We Are not Alone*, but we have to act as though we were unique.

If any one of us were to wake up some morning with a bright and complete plan for the future of the entire human race, he would be wise to consult a psychiatrist before going ahead with it. It is certain, however, that there is no such plan in sight at the moment, anywhere, at any organizational or governmental level.

For instance, our own and other countries are not preparing for a clearly possible technological utopia. We are all preparing, to the best of our abilities, for something we hope and try to believe won't happen—a nuclear war.

III

Preparing: for What?

I DO NOT suggest that our country should lay down its arms while other nations continue to construct and maintain them. The nuclear nations are all caught in the same trap. So long as we fail to trust one another we shall arm against one another. And modern peace-time armament, when it includes nuclear weapons, costs more than old-fashioned war.

The current budget for the United States Government earmarks about half of all expenditures for defense. About one-sixth as much goes for what is called Health, Education, and Welfare—a new Department. Some persons, on the basis of this fraction, call us a welfare state. If expenditures mean anything, we are more likely to become a military state—a garrison state.

I don't detect any signs of military arrogance as I go about the country. No officers in uniform elbow me off the sidewalk. The force that pushes me around is in well-chosen civilian clothes; it is a tax collector. I pay my taxes as cheerfully as I can, but I wonder. Shall *we* stop preparing for "defense" when *they* don't? That is the tormenting question of the day.

There have never been any good arguments at all for the war system. There are fewer than there were, with the arrival of the newest weapon. War never proved anything, except that one side was stronger or more determined than the other. Or less scrupulous. Now war is like going over Niagara in a barrel—futile and almost certainly suicidal.

Little wars can and do still occur, as in Korea, the Congo, Vietnam, and Palestine. Of our last two big wars, the first cost about five million lives from all nations, mostly of soldiers killed or dead in service; the second took about twenty million lives, including civilians killed in bombing raids or foully murdered by the German Nazis.

The French General Joffre, a solid, plodding type with something less than Napoleonic genius, was once asked what his strategy was. "I nibble them," he replied, blandly overlooking the fact that the Germans were also nibbling at their enemies.

The Second World War was not of the nibbling sort. And now? What are we preparing for? What are the major Powers of the earth, the United States among them, preparing for?

2.

The conventional weapon still has, I suppose, an honorable place in hell, but it could not be a weapon of final survival in a major conflict. I do not mean to belittle conventional ways of killing persons. Land mines, bayonets, swords, flame throwers, explosives filled with jellied gasoline, buzz bombs such as the Germans fired indiscriminately into London, the Allied "fire bombs" that produced "fire storms" in one or two German cities—all these are still worthy of notice. The atom bomb is not a bit more cruel; it is merely, as I was saying, more efficient.

The individual victim suffers no more pain when this weapon is used instead of the familiar old-fashioned instruments of death; it is the community that suffers, it is the nation, it is mankind, it is the goodness and graciousness of normal civilization.

The question arises, are we and our neighbors preparing for the old-fashioned type of war, or for the new-fashioned, or for both? One is not told the answer. One may deduce it.

3.

I share the dense ignorance of nearly all tax-paying and voting citizens. We cannot take our muskets and go down to Concord Bridge. We do not know what is going on. Nor do we know what ought to go on. As far as I can make out, the Defense Department does not know the answer, either. Shall we rely, for example, chiefly on the atomic weapon? Or shall we depend mainly on the dear old explosives we are used to, while keeping the ultimate weapon up to date and ready for business? The indications are that we are trying to do both these things, hoping that we can somehow find the money to pay for both activities. At this writing, the war in Vietnam, like that in Korea, is mostly of the old style, not much ahead in technique of the Second World War.

Our leaders let us know, by accident and design, that they do have innovations up their sleeves. A military plane is wrecked near a Spanish shore; it turns out to have been carrying armed atom bombs. We are allowed to hear of atom bombs being carried around in submarines, ready for use if needed, and planted in "silos," already aimed at possible targets.

What are we preparing for? Not, certainly, for Gettysburg, St. Mihiel, the Normandy landing, or Okinawa. To defend our country? Yes. By what strategy? The strategists won't tell us. We wouldn't tell if we were they, for secrecy is half the battle.

A consideration of the history of war doesn't help us much. The military effort has always been to break the enemy's will to resist, sometimes by killing him, sometimes by humiliating him or scaring him. In former times he could be sold into slavery, or if important enough, held for ransom. A modern refinement is the rules for the humane treatment of prisoners. If enough prisoners are taken there isn't any war any more.

The means for bringing about these results are familiar to most of us. Commanding officers have always learned the art of war by getting their men killed and wounded; the famous generals, the geniuses in that sad specialty, are those who learned fastest with the least cost to their own troops.

For military men, technicians, and manufacturers, the conventional types of warfare are always the most convenient; one has only to do his homework, study the state of the industrial arts, allow for a few new gadgets, and one is ready for something closely resembling the last war.

In the art of war this has always been so. The profession of killing has slowly but steadily improved. The Macedonian phalanx, the Roman legion within its fortified camp, the British square—each has been followed by something a little better but not drastically different. The Carthaginians even had a tank, though they called it an elephant. Weapons developed in the same gradual fashion. The catapult was followed by gunpowder-powered artillery. The musket was replaced by the more accurate rifle, the single-shot weapon by the machine gun, cavalry by airplanes, sailing ships of wood by steamships armored in steel, small guns by bigger ones. In some naval battles of the Second World War the opposing ships never saw one another, which made tactics markedly different from those used in Nelson's times, when the crews sometimes grappled with the enemy and boarded his ship.

Infantry tactics changed, too. Generals in the Second World War had to learn all over again what Grant had discovered during our own Civil War, that it is bloody murder to attack defended lines with dense masses of infantry.

The brightest military men were as busy as bees thinking up improvements to make war more effective and interesting, although the numerous dull generals seemed to hanker to have the days of knighthood and the Crusades back again. The trouble was, of course, that one couldn't long have a new invention all to himself. The British in the First World War were first with tanks, but these vehicles were standard equipment before the war was over. Since then the so-called cavalry has gone clankety-clank instead of ploppity-plop, and has had much less fresh air.

War developed like the factory system, only more slowly—military men are usually more conservative than manufacturers. No general would have invented the assembly line. But war did in fact develop, in a perfectly normal, predictable way, and has done so down to the moment at which I am writing. A veteran of the Second World War would have found some things new to him in Korea, and a Korean veteran some things new to him in Vietnam, but these were like differences in motor cars. A man who could drive an automobile in 1934 could still drive one in 1964 if he were still young enough. And the same with fighting tools.

We have been developing better fighting tools, of the conventional sort, right along. So have other nations. The newer ones are quieter running, with easier acceleration and more automatic features, but I imagine they are perceptably descended from those used in earlier warfare.

Our own government is spending great sums of money on these things. If it did not do so it would have only one weapon—the atomic one, which it earnestly desires never to use.

But it spends great sums on the atomic weapons, too. Several other nations do the same. These are what are known as deterrents.

Our own nation and others, therefore, now have a double defense bill: one part to pay the cost of fighting a normal, old-fashioned war; the other to make atomic weapons to discourage other nations from using their atomic weapons.

This atomic weapon is manifestly nothing that Attila, Hannibal, Napoleon, von Moltke, or U. S. Grant would think of. It is not the kind of irrationality to which they were accustomed. It is an entirely new and infinitely more horrible fantasy of the human mind.

We have to buy it. But I cannot imagine a professional soldier taking much pleasure in it.

4.

The critical question is, what are we buying? What are we preparing for—or against? I should say we are preparing *for* the old-fashioned kind of combat, piously hoping not to become involved in it, though regarding it as fairly probable for a nation that has undertaken the responsibility of policing half the world. We can stand this kind of war, though it is expensive to get ready for and expensive to fight.

We are preparing *against* what we devoutly pray will not happen—atomic war. This is not war at all in the old-fashioned sense. It has no attraction, even for the most eager of military men, nor the most enterprising of manufacturers of military hardware.

But each of these two kinds of preparedness is hideously costly, although one is intended to meet an emergency and the other is thought of as insurance against catastrophe. It is a coincidence that these two entirely separate things are regarded as part of the national defense. We have no Department of Aggression, nor do I believe that since 1898 we have ever intended or committed aggression.

Our preparedness position is exactly what the governments of all other nations pretend to profess. Hitler was probably the last ruler to send troops across another nation's boundary in an explicit attempt to get more territory. Even the Chinese communists are not as frank as that; they merely infiltrate for doctrinal reasons or to come to the aid, as they profess, of peoples struggling for liberty.

Under these circumstances, atomic defense may be rational from each nation's point of view, but regarded as a collective activity of the human race, it is a self-destroying madness.

We can say that we did our best to end this nightmare when we offered, in 1946, to internationalize and in fact socialize nuclear weapons. Russia, the leader of world communism, refused this almost Marxian proposal. The race to spend the most money and risk the most lives thus was made to continue.

One effect of this competition was to release into the neutral and embattled air, quantities of radioactive debris. We therefore made an agreement with the Russians to do nuclear testing underground. Maybe they have complied. We have not always been sure.

The competition itself did not end. France has now engaged in it, as has Communist China. So much can be done with the weapons already on hand that I cannot see the use of new experiments. But the experts, who know so much and tell us ignorant laymen so little, are still seeking perfection.

So there we stand. Any nuclear Power could, as the saying goes, "take out" New York, Washington, and other key American cities; we in our turn could take out that Power's key cities almost simultaneously. This is one of the gifts of the gods we are paying taxes for. Hitler asked, in one of his final hours, "Is Paris burning?" I wonder if we would take comfort, as we sat among the ruins, to know that Berlin, Moscow, or Peking was burning. Or in the swift thought, as the stars rushed downward, as well they might, that it would not be necessary to pay that third installment on our federal income tax.

This may sound like science fiction, although those who are experts in the field of nuclear weapons and those who were fortunate or unfortunate enough to survive what happened at Hiroshima and Nagasaki may feel differently.

My own opinion, which I think many humble observers of the state of the world today may share, is that if we continue to conduct our disputes with arms of any sort we will in time bring the nuclear bomb into circulation and that most of us will subsequently have little to worry about—or with.

This is why I turn to the United Nations, not as a product of wistful and sentimental thinking, but as an absolute necessity if modern civilization is to survive.

IV

·······

The International Fire Department

THE UNITED NATIONS Charter was drawn up and signed, in San Francisco in the spring of 1945, before the existence of an atomic bomb was generally known. It was explicitly designed to guard against the old-fashioned kind of war. But if this had not happened at that time and place it would have had to happen later. The bomb, which would have to wait about four months off-stage, was frightful beyond all previous imaginings, but it was a great conciliator.

The U. N. differs from all previous organizations for peace in that it is an outgrowth of necessity rather than an expression of a purely altruistic aspiration. In this light I would like to take a look at it.

It is no haven of pure good will. At its New York headquarters, for example, the most casual visitor may observe that the representatives of the Arab States do not speak to those from Israel, nor the Israeli to them. Similarly the Russians have had nothing to do with the Nationalist

49

Chinese, whom they regard as imposters and not Chinese at all. The Soviets may differ with the Peking Chinese, but when it comes to voting in the U. N. they regard them as the only genuine Chinese anywhere around. No communist member of the U. N. has ever looked upon the Taiwan Government as the legitimate spokesman for China. Practically, it is hard to see how it could be, however much one's sympathies may turn toward it.

But these are the attitudes and problems of individual nations, not those of the United Nations. The Taiwan Chinese may be snubbed, but in the U. N. enclave they cannot be pushed around. Nor can Israel. I would like to believe that tommorow's communities all over the earth will be as free from discrimination as the U. N., by its basic laws, has to be and is; no nation, race, or creed can be treated here as inferior to any other. There is a restaurant to which delegates may invite their friends: the dark, the light, the yellow, the members from democracies and from dictatorships, the men (and often women, too) from the small as well as the large countries—all will be welcomed here, in the order of their appearance or of their reservations.

There is one bit of discrimination that may enlighten our Southern, South African, or Rhodesian contemporaries: since the general public is admitted only after the needs of the delegates have been met, a white visitor may have to wait until a Negro delegate and his friends have finished their meal.

The guards are expected to be, and are, as polite to the delegates from Salvador or Liberia as they are to those from the giant monoliths—the United States and Soviet Russia. France does not take precedence over the delegate from her former province of Mauritania.

Social equality inside the U. N. does not, to be sure, imply political equality, just as in our own country Rhode Island does not swing as much weight as New York or California. By the U. N. Charter, the great Powers have a permanent membership and a perpetual veto in the Security Council. The elective members of the Council cannot out-vote even one of them on what is termed a "substantive" question.

The power of little Taiwan is that it is technically the spokesman for about seven hundred million Chinese—not merely the twelve million or so it actually governs. Taiwan has not abused this power, for it is in fact dependent on American backing. But whatever the background facts, the rules define its powers as though it were in truth one of the mighty national forces of the earth.

I observed the U. N. journalistically for many years, from its foundation at San Francisco in 1945; I attended its tenth-year and twentieth-year commemoration meetings in that city; I have followed its wanderings around Greater New York, before it settled at its monumental slab-and-dome headquarters on Manhattan's East River; I have also visited the impressive Geneva structures where some of its agencies function, and the massive office buildings of the Food and Agriculture Organization in Rome, Italy. In this way I have had the chance to pass among groups and gatherings of delegates as an innocent and in a sense invis-ible bystander. Today there are fewer foreign costumes than there used to be, but the reality of a clash and meeting of cultures has persisted over the years.

Some old-fashioned diplomats may find this embarrassing; I think some of these would like something resembling the Congress of Berlin in 1878, which unwittingly but in a most decorous manner laid the foundations for the World Wars of 1914–18 and 1939–45. But that drama is played out. Its diplomacy was as spurious as that of a huddle of monkeys dividing a pile of coconuts, or of a gang of mutually suspicious bank robbers dividing the loot. Imperialism is dying hard, but dying it is—in spite of the fact that communist spokesmen are fond of calling all Western nations imperialist. The power struggle will remain for a while, but that is a different thing. Imperialism died because it didn't pay any more, just as feudalism died some centuries earlier.

Nor are there any quaint and pliable little peoples any more—there are merely governments that control limited areas. And these no-longer-humble little nations are discovering at the U. N. that in union (or alliances, or understandings, or sometimes a bit of horse trading) there is strength.

2.

Once, in the hot summer of 1919, I saw the back of Woodrow Wilson's head. This great and tragic President was then engaged in trying to get the Senate to ratify the Treaty of Versailles. This document contained the settlements of the First World War, some of them blundering, ignorant, and cynical. It also included the Covenant of the League of Nations. I was in Washington trying to find out, for a New York newspaper, what was happening and why.

I got as far as the office of Mr. Tumulty, then Mr.

Wilson's chief secretary. Why Mr. Tumulty should have invited me to come that far when he knew the President would not have time to see me I don't know. I sat at Mr. Tumulty's desk for a few minutes, and through an open door I saw Mr. Wilson's head—or part of it. I had the audacity to think that if the President had been more patient with those Senators who suggested mild reservations, he could have put his country into the League. I had talked with several Senators, who had gotten into a mood where anything that Mr. Wilson wanted they emphatically didn't want. I talked with Borah, who was less vindictive but just as determined. I had interviewed several middle-of-the-roaders. If I had been older and perhaps if I had represented more circulation I might have been allowed to report, present the arguments I had been listening to, and even ask the President a few questions.

But I suppose Mr. Wilson was trying to do something the country wasn't ready for. The wild men in the Senate, and some of the tamer ones, bogged down on the foolish and unworkable parts of the peace settlement and also on Article Ten of the Covenant. And what did Article Ten do? It bound the signatories to some sort of action if an unprovoked aggression took place.

Our people didn't even want to promise to consider action, much less take any. They had, as the saying went, had it. They were tired of war. They were disillusioned by what they had heard of the motives behind the settlement imposed by the victors at Versailles. Was it for this that young men had rotted on the wire of the old Western Front? Our people did not wish to be dragged into any more European entanglements—and for about twenty-two and a half years they were not.

The treaty was defeated. Male babies born in that year, 1919, would be shot down in the Normandy Landing, but how could any prophet—especially a United States Senator of the old school—foresee that? Harding, the next President after Wilson, called for "an association of nations," though he never did anything about it and apparently never intended to. Mr. Coolidge, who unexpectedly succeeded Mr. Harding, did not bother to promise; he probably calculated nobody would believe him if he did, which was unquestionably true.

So we had a nice, cosy little country of our own. George Washington or Thomas Jefferson or somebody had warned us to avoid entangling alliances. We did so. Then we had a big boom and a big depression, which occupied our attention for about a decade.

Yet the thought of some sort of alliance to keep the peace did not die out. It had been in men's minds ever since the Greeks organized what they called the Amphitryonic League to protect their temples. Grotius in the seventeenth century tried to prevent war or at least humanize it. He did not succeed, though his name became famous.

But organizations and movements to prevent war kept cropping up. They were never more numerous or more active than just before the First World War. Andrew Carnegie was so interested that he took time from endowing libraries to start a Peace Foundation.

3.

But the idea of a world union for peace struck terror into the hearts of our bravest statesmen. So we did not enter the League of Nations. We did not commit ourselves, even in the most cautious way, to doing one-tenth of one percent as much as the fates later compelled us to do. Our leaders, after Wilson, refused for many years to look further than the ends of their noses. They would not even let us join that alarming institution, the Court of International Justice, as it was then called. Nobody, we vowed, would catch us playing around with the bad boys down at the corner drugstore.

Franklin D. Roosevelt, pondering the situation in his own way and considering some facts not available in 1919, talked with an old friend with whom he often but not always agreed (a Mr. Churchill), and came to a few conclusions.

One of these conclusions was that the League's proposed successor, the United Nations, must not be set up as part of the peace treaty. When it was signed, at the end of June, 1945, Mr. Roosevelt was dead, the war with Germany was over, and the war with Japan was still going on. The U. N. was above the battle.

Another of Mr. Roosevelt's conclusions was that the American people would now be willing to give up the policy of isolation, for the simple reason that they had tried it and it just wouldn't work.

A third conclusion was that this was a Big Power world, and that if any of the Big Powers were to go to war with one or more other Big Powers the jig was up. The subsequent unveiling of the A-bomb underlined this statement.

With this sweeping exception, the Security Council was empowered, as a last resort, to "take such action by sea, air, or land forces as may be necessary to maintain or restore international peace and security." In practice, this clause gave the Great Powers authority to coerce any weaker nations who were committing breaches of the peace—providing the Great Powers unanimously wanted to. Since they rarely wanted anything unanimously, the coercive authority could come into force only by accident—as it did when Russia walked out of the Security Council shortly before the Korean crisis.

The Russians did not put the Security Council veto over on the ingenuous Americans; we wanted it just as much and just as shrewdly as they did, though we have seldom used it. What the Russians did get that they were not entitled to was three votes in the Assembly, on the theory that the Ukraine and Bielorussia were separate and independent republics—a notable stretching of the truth. But President Truman, like President Roosevelt, was a practical man; he wanted and got a Charter that the Russians would sign and our own Senate would ratify.

The Charter gives evidence of having been produced while the world was still in a state of shock. The war had been the most destructive in history. And Hitler, who wanted it and caused it, had not done this horrible thing all by himself: he had had the aid of imaginative inventors, careful technicians and contractors who designed, built, and made money out of the gas chambers; he had reached down into the primeval slime and brought up monsters who were only too happy to operate that lethal machinery. In short, the massive Nazi crimes were planned and carried out by an entire legion of the damned; they were not an accident and not the impulsive act of a single perverted individual. We could afford to sacrifice a degree of sovereignty to prevent that sort of thing from recurring.

The Japanese had been treacherous and cruel, too, though they had not carried out a previously planned policy of extermination. Hitler and his bloodthirsty guttersnipes (to borrow an apt phrase from the late Winston Churchill) had committed a deed so horrible that the most cynical of delegates at San Francisco were appalled. They gazed into the morass of depravity and drew back.

They did all they thought they could, under the strong emotions of the moment. At the same time they preferred not to give one another any special powers or advantages —as is a routine precaution among allies. They made the Charter a more practicable instrument than the League Covenant had been. What was not obviously practicable simply was not attempted. Some things were tried and dropped. The ambitious project for a Military Staff Committee, with which all members were to cooperate, gradually faded out. As nearly as I can ascertain the Russians talked it to death.

The A-bomb, let alone the H-bomb, was not mentioned in the Charter. It was still in rehearsal, still top-secret, still not a known part of the future, and so could not get into the debates. Therefore, all plans for keeping the peace or restoring the peace, were still of the old-fashioned or "conventional" sort when the delegates at San Francisco lined up to sign the book.

The document contained some hypocrisy, some eloquently noble language, and some common sense. I like to re-read its opening lines: "We, the people of the United Nations, determined to save succeeding generations from the scourge of war [this phrase may have been lifted from Lincoln's Second Inaugural], which twice in our life-time has brought untold sorrow to mankind; and to reaffirm faith in fundamental human rights, in the dignity and worth of the human person, in the equal rights of men and women and of nations large and small . . ." This documentary prose had and still has a power to stir men's hearts.

Some of those present may not have had the slightest intention of living up to the noble sentiments expressed, but they signed just the same. There was and is no Court that could determine accurately what is "the dignity and worth of the human person." What of it? The words were there: for the major Powers a commendable resolution, for the smaller nations a plea against injustice. The dictum that "all men are created equal" was put into our own Declaration of Independence by the votes of slave owners, and after nearly two hundred years it is still not fully realized; nevertheless it has deeply influenced our laws and our thinking.

The Charter was declared ratified on October 24, 1945. The first General Assembly met in London in January, 1946. It took up business where the old League of Nations had petered out.

4.

I first saw the League briefly in action when it was occupying an old wooden hotel in Geneva, in the spring of 1927. The Secretary-General of that date was a soft-spoken, rather discouraged Englishman. I talked with him, then attended a commitee hearing where the subject was the illicit trade in opium. Later the League moved into some imposing new buildings, which the U. N. subsequently took over, and which my wife and I visited twenty-odd years afterward.

The most pathetic League of Nations building I ever saw was a small one—hardly more than a kiosque—at the New York World's Fair in 1939. This one was not sad because it was so small, but because so few persons paid any attention to it and because the League was so manifestly at its last gasp. Russia, in an act of perfidy notable even in diplomatic records, had just made an alliance with Hitler's Germany.

The young ladies at the League hut or hovel at the New York World's Fair wore brave, forced smiles. They also gave out literature. The League's only diplomatic triumph, as I recall, had been the Aland Islands settlement between Sweden and Finland, neither of which countries wanted a war. The League had also taken care of refugees, had been an instrument in the population interchanges between Greece and Turkey, and had negotiated hundreds of international agreements in non-political areas—for instance, one for charting and regulating the world's lighthouses. It could be, and was, a useful instrument. But it could not prevent wars, except between minor Powers who were not in a military mood. The Great Powers remained free to do as they deemed wise.

The most courageous thing the League did was to impose mild "sanctions" on Mussolini when he decided to attack Ethiopia; Mussolini said that he would never forgive this. The League was careful, however, not to put an embargo on any war materials Mussolini really needed, nor to interfere with the passage of his transports through the Suez Canal, which Britain and France then controlled.

When the Japanese invaded North China, the League obtained an excellent report from Lord Lytton's Commission
(1932) recommending sanctions—but nothing was done.

Neither the separate nations nor the League of Nations
had ever felt strong enough to act, or even to speak forc-
ibly when Hitler re-militarized the Rhineland, which Germany had promised not to do; nor when he took the Sude-
tenland, Austria, and Czechoslovakia—just as a smaller-
scale burglar might have made away with a bride's flat
silver.

Now let us turn over some pages in the calendar. The
United Nations, which in 1945 replaced the League, has a
more resolute voice than the League ever had, and a greater
ability to act. It has already outlasted the League, which
had an effective duration of a little over twenty years.

As time has gone by the U. N. has lost some of its original self-consciousness and tenseness, and has settled into
what might be called a predictable routine. A Russian delegate now feels free to proceed to its halls and corridors
without the old flying-wedge formation his predecessors
used. Delegates who are on speaking terms have come to
know each other better. Personages have been sent to the
New York City meetings who would never have dreamed
of wasting their time in the old League debates.

The emotions that boiled through chambers and ante-
rooms in U. N.'s early days may not have decreased, but
their expression has become almost a routine. The day
came when I sat in the press gallery at the Manhattan
Headquarters and realized that I was acutely bored. For
me, one of the anonymous three billion inhabitants of this
great globe, this was a historic occasion. I knew now that

the U. N., like Congress and the jury system, was a success. Delegates were walking in and out during meetings, just as they do on Capitol Hill in Washington.

At the same time, each speaker, especially if he came from an obscure and diminutive country, was anxious to express himself, to have his entire speech—every blessed word of it—put into the record, to be exposed to the television cameras, shining redly from certain stage boxes, in brief, to have his own and his country's day in court. Individual as well as national egos and personalities were on show, in a fashion. The U. N. had little real power, but it did receive publicity. It was news—not the self-inflicted tedium that the League had become in its last days.

There had been much debate and deliberation as to where its headquarters should be located. Sites as wide apart as Fairfield County, Connecticut, and San Francisco had been mentioned. The final choice, on Manhattan's East River, was admirable, for New York was already the most international of cities. It became simple for American and foreign newspapers, as well as the television and radio circuits, to cover the proceedings. The buildings became a place of pilgrimage for out-of-town and foreign visitors, including multitudes of school children who were brought in buses from many miles around. The U. N. has been made known to millions of people, as the old League never was. An observer at the U. N. could be conscious of a world press, a world diplomacy, and a world public opinion in a way that had never been possible before.

The diplomats and the press met to some extent in the Delegates' Restaurant or in one of the Delegates' Lounges. I never saw any excessive drinking during working hours but there were convenient opportunities for loosening up. The bartenders, I often thought, knew more about what went on at the U. N. than most newspapermen—and of course, bound by the ethics of their profession, revealed less.

There were also the great receptions and cocktail parties, ordinarily held away from the Headquarters Building. Some of these were dense with persons one didn't mind meeting. It was quite a circus. I don't believe even Washington could match it.

There were some intimate social events, of course, for delegates from countries that were on easy speaking terms with one another. Newspapermen sometimes got into these. Nobody starved, either for food or for information.

It will be evident that though the U. N. had a fairly stiff official life of its own, as set down in the Charter and various rules for procedure, it also had the social aspects of a true world capital. The U. N. was, and I assume still is, human. It is a living and growing institution, not a piece of machinery. It is made up of individuals as well as of nations, and whatever the instructions that may roll in from various foreign offices, there is a great range of striking personalities.

5.

The U. N. has been growing. It took its first bow at San Francisco with delegates from fifty prospective members present. One more, Poland, signed during the Charter year. As I write there are 117 members, but every now and then a small tract of formerly dependent real estate is set free, runs up a new flag, and asks to join the club.

The result is that the power balance has changed in the General Assembly, where each member, large or small, has one vote. Decisions of this body on questions regarded as "substantive" require a two-thirds majority of members present and voting. In the early days the United States had enough adherents and allies, in Latin America and elsewhere, to clamp a veto—one-third plus one—on any proposal it did not like.

This was unspeakably convenient, and especially so when a question had been abstracted from a deadlocked Security Council and transferred by a handy parliamentary subterfuge to the Assembly. But a small minority of humanity, measured in population, can now block the will of the vast majority—ourselves included. This difficulty might be diminished by amending the Charter so that Assembly votes might be weighted according to the populations behind them. But amendment of the Charter requires the votes of two-thirds of the Assembly and all the permanent members of the Security Council.

And there are other difficulties. Suppose mainland China gets in with a vote weighted according to its population?

My own opinion is that whatever the urgency, there will be no major change in the U. N. for quite a while. Neither will the U. N. wither away, as the League did. The smaller nations don't dare to face the future without it. The Great Powers could exist without it, but they would have to establish new lines of communication to replace it. They have always recognized its importance by sending important diplomats to its meetings—even, to one historic session, Khrushchev, Tito, and a representative of power politics, though not of a Great Power, Castro. Our own long-term representatives, Henry Cabot Lodge, the late Adlai E. Stevenson, and former Justice Arthur E. Goldberg of the Supreme Court, have had and deserved cabinet rank.

Within the U. N. itself there have been three eminent Secretaries-General: Trygve Lie, Dag Hammarskjöld, and U Thant. Mr. Hammarskjöld was probably one of the great men of the century; he would spend an hour or two in meditation in a California redwood grove; he was also reported to be able to stand up to the Russians, in private, and scold them as though they were naughty children.

The powers of the Secretary-General, in moral terms, are shattering. Hitler said of the Pope: "How many divisions has he?" The answer would be the same if the same question were asked about this unique international official; he has many divisions and many banners. Nobody else in the world can so effectively defend the rights of all humanity—and in particular the rights of those who cannot effectively defend themselves.

The U. N. will endure, I believe, for two reasons: first, because it is a handy means of communication; second, because it is a handy forum and gathering place. As I leaf through my English constitutional history I note that at the end of the thirteenth century King Edward I was *summoning* representatives to Parliament—he wanted to extract tax money from them. Out of the English kings' need of money grew all the parliaments of the world, although in time the ruling monarch in England called and dissolved Parliament as the ministers instructed her to do, and got money only as Parliament desired. The U. N., necessary now for purposes at least as utilitarian as Edward's were, may likewise go beyond its original mandate.

Meanwhile, the troops don't march. There need be no accidental wars. No ambitious general has a chance to win fame at the cost of other men's lives. The U. N. has had many bitter but not bloody squabbles.

6.

Then there are what are officially called the Specialized Agencies—more informally, the Non-Governmental Organizations or N. G. O.'s. These, many of them inherited from the League, are engaged in good works and nothing else. They are political only in the sense that they sometimes interfere with persons, organizations, and even governments that are engaged in bad works.

There are fourteen such agencies at this writing, all of them committed to "wide international responsibilities . . . in economic, social, cultural, educational, health, and related fields" (I quote Article 57 of the U. N. Charter). All report to U. N. through the Economic and Social Council.

I shan't list these organizations, nor try to tell all that they do. Dip in almost at random: the Food and Agriculture Organization works to increase the world's food supply; the World Health Organization is raising the level of humanity's health; the International Labor Organization is attempting, among other things, to promote social justice; the U. N. Educational, Scientific, and Cultural Organization tries to "further human rights" in various ways. There are agencies for the promotion of the peaceful uses of the atom, for international development, for carrying the mails and for child health.

A statement of intent has of course no saving grace. But

those who have watched these benevolent institutions have found in them a great earnestness in well-doing. The N. G. O.'s have their jealousies, their differences of opinion, their human weaknesses, but I believe those who direct them are among the world's most compassionate men and women. Here, if anywhere, the voice of civilization speaks.

These organizations may in the end intensify the fearful problem I have mentioned earlier—a massive increase in population. But must we suppress our compassion for the sick, the hungry, the young, and the elderly in order to prevent over-crowding? I can't make myself think so. There are other and kindlier ways.

As I look at all these phases of the U. N., I like to think that a small and helpless person or a small and feeble nation, exposed to all the winds that blow, may some day come naturally to the U. N. for protection. I believe this happened in Korea. I believe it happened, notwithstanding all the bloodshed and turmoil, in the Congo.

The time has surely passed when an aggressive nation may pick up any piece of outlying territory it desires—and to which no other and perhaps stronger Power lays claim —without asking permission. Words such as peace, security, equality, justice may not be self-operative, no matter how well they sound in a speech; yet if there is a forum where they can be uttered, if they go like flames throughout the earth, they will rally a strength that may make them prevail.

What we have on the East River and in related buildings in Geneva, Rome, and on a smaller scale elsewhere, wherever a U. N. "presence" plants its flag, is a continuously operative international front. The Security Council, in theory if not always in fact, "is organized so as to be able to function continuously." The Assembly not only holds regular sessions once a year but it may be called upon "in such special sessions as occasion may require." The greater the emergency the swifter the action. The buildings, the secretarial apparatus, truly international in intent if not always in fact, are always there—a valiant symbol against the sky.

If the major Powers are sanely resolved to talk rather than fight, the U. N. can pounce on any threat to "peace and security."

7.

Sentimentality has helped to create and sustain the U. N., but cannot of itself save it. At its best the U. N. is a medicine for a sick world. It is an inoculation against the disease of war—and not a perfect one at that. Its available means and resources are still inadequate. It has not been able to prevent secondary wars in Korea, the Congo, and Vietnam, though it operated in the first two of these and has offered its negotiating facilities in the third.

It is not a world union, much less a world state. Some of its members have successfully withstood pressure to make them pay their share for police operations voted in the Assembly—as in Palestine and the Congo. The U. N. is weaker than the old American Confederation of revolutionary days, which could do hardly anything but pass resolutions; the Confederation could call for troops but could not raise them, could ask for money but had no power to collect it from the unwilling.

The U. N. is as strong, nevertheless, as the present state

of civilization will permit it to be. It is useless to demand a powerful world federation until the governments involved are willing to give up some of what they call their sovereignty. Ultimately they will be frightened into doing this, or driven to it by cold reason, just as the former American colonists were in 1787. We must hope, dream—and be patient.

Meanwhile, something has been accomplished. The U. N. has made it harder for any government to get away with the Hitler species of the Big Lie. The pretences that were humbly accepted at Munich and Berchtesgaden would not be effective today. The protests of the weak would reverberate throughout the world.

V

....

The Happy Isles

MY EARLIER chapters have dealt with some fairly serious, not to say ominous, subjects. Suppose we want to get away from them all. From it all, in fact. Islands, chiefly of the Pacific variety, come into our minds. The wind in the palm trees. The long surf breaking on the outer reef. Natives singing and dancing every night; a full moon at all times. That sort of thing.

The cruise ships do indeed stop at them, and it is pleasant to go ashore and see if anybody is combing the beaches in the old-fashioned way. Nobody is. Nobody goes to the South Seas any more to get away from it all. What is here is there, too, though the language may be different.

Not that these places are crowded, except around the big ports. There is quite a lot of open space in the State of Hawaii, especially in the outer islands. The same with such retreats as Tahiti and Samoa. In the middle of Australia, which may be thought of as a big island, is a location called Alice Springs, where traffic is no problem.

But do not be deceived by the legend that anything on earth is remote any more. (We shall approach this subject

again in a later chapter.) If you ride around a big ocean in a
ship, or over the same on an airplane, you can go ashore for
a little while, buy your curios, have a good time, drink the
local rum, watch the natives—if any—dance; but do not
look for the ancient miracle of mystery and illusion. Who
is isolated from what in these days? If nothing else happens,
a man comes along with a transistor.

Does this sound depressing? Probably not to anybody
born after 1920. It is a part of the future. Of course you
can stay aboard the ship or out at the airfield and watch
those palms, and drink more than is good for you. But this
is a subterfuge.

There are palms in the United States, including those
that have to be greased frequently. Also rum. Also steel
guitars. Let us wipe away our tears and inspect the facts
clearly.

2.

At least one South Sea island isn't there any more; we
blew it up with an H-bomb—and everybody was sur-
prised, including the scientists who directed the explosion.
The Pacific, North and South, also became a sort of target
range; it is safe and agreeable to travel there if you keep out
of the firing lanes. A nation says, we intend to shoot from
somewhere to a portion of the Great Ice Barrier; we will
do this at ten A.M. next Thursday, and please keep out of
the way. Otherwise the Pacific, if you keep far enough
away from its western continental shores, is still as pacific
as can be. In certain seasons and areas it may kick up a
typhoon, but this is nothing new—it has always done that.

Our motives in what we do in this watery area are admittedly lofty; when we shoot along the Pacific range or send up an H-bomb on an island, we do this to protect Akron, Ohio. Others do it to protect their own cities. Nobody has any aggressive intentions, so it is stated. But these experiments turn the vast expanses of the ocean into a small lake, even more effectively than do the swift passage of airplanes. (This is another topic we'll come to later.)

Perhaps the present generation does not understand what a remote Pacific island used to be like. It was never, perhaps, what we oldsters (youngsters then) imagined it. But there were, and still are, two kinds of Pacific islands, the high ones, such as Tahiti, and the low ones, such as—shall I say?—the atoll called Bikini. There was and is Easter Island, with its huge, brooding stone figures. There was Pitcairn Island, where the mutineers of the *Bounty* took refuge; they could not have been safer from what the British naval martinets regarded as justice if they had landed on the moon. There was and is, again, Tahiti, where Melville jumped ship and Gauguin painted; and where Nordhoff and Hall, battle-weary veterans of World War I, did some good writing. Tahiti is hardly secluded from the outer world any more. Nor is Stevenson's Samoa.

The other islands are still there, too. In fact, once in a while a volcanic eruption throws a new one up, though it is sensible to wait a while before going aboard. But it isn't islands that we lack, it isn't wilderness, even; it is isolation that is missing.

Think of a world in which Marco Polo could go traveling around beyond the back of the beyond and come home surfeited with gold and wonders; or in which Sir John Mandeville could compile stories of journeys into unsuspected places, including one country in which men carried their heads out of harm's way, under their arms; or in which Columbus' sailors really and truly thought they might come to a place where the earth would end; or Peary slogging to the North Pole and Amundsen to the South Pole, neither one quite sure what to look for.

Think, even, of a time when the best route from the Missouri River to the Pacific Ocean was not known, and when parties plodded day after day toward the mysterious ranges (the Shining Mountains, some called them), sometimes finding wonders such as Yellowstone and the Great Salt Lake. And the days when a sailing ship would make a dim landfall at twilight and coast back and forth all night long, waiting for the morning star and the sign of a safe harbor, no one knowing what this island was or what manner of man inhabited it.

The patience of men, the lust for riches, the restlessness, the hardihood have now solved all the spatial geographical problems. Beyond the horizon there will always be, as we now know, more of the same. Our unsated curiosity now turns inward, into the inconceivably small, and outward, into immeasurable distances, but the surface of our planet we know almost too well. It has no more surprises for us.

There is, of course, a great deal still to be learned about the earth. The profundities of the sea are being explored, but the process is slow and far from completed. It will take infinite patience to work out the contours under all the oceans as accurately as the U. S. Geological Survey has done for the land area of the United States and the Coast and Geodetic Survey for our off-shore soundings.

Almost everyone has seen topographic maps of parts of

this planet's surface. The Army needs them, of course, and domestic hikers carry them in their packs. The series for this country was not quite complete the last time I looked into the matter, but it can easily be made so, now that we can take reliable photographs from the air.

But this isn't the sort of gamble that exhilarated Magellan's men when they sailed among the Spice Islands. Today Magellan would find a galvanized iron roof, a group of foot-sore tourists, a few empty Cola bottles and phonograph records of last year's Broadway musical shows on any one of the islands.

We all used to know the line from *The Ancient Mariner:* "We were the first that ever burst into that silent sea." Today there are no silent seas into which any of us can be the first to burst.

That is all over. There are no kingdoms of Prester John, no gardens of Kublai Khan, no Johnsonian Valley of Rasselas, Prince of Abyssinia; the Gardens of the Hesperides are no more; Atlantis has sunk beneath the waves and will not emerge again. The only places we cannot go, even if we have the money for the tickets, are those where the communist or other governments have military secrets or have made mistakes so depressing they dare not let us see them. These places would not be especially romantic, anyhow.

We can still fall back on imagined utopias, but I believe few of us do this any more. Certainly we can no longer indicate their dreamed-of location, in some remote and mysterious quarter of the earth. The magic of distance is dead.

3.

The glories of the first Elizabethan Age grew out of the sudden realization that the earth was man's and the fullness thereof, that improbable things could happen, that Englishmen and possibly others could go anywhere and do anything.

There will be no second period like this, not even for those who walk around the dark side of the moon. Where now is Prospero's Isle?

Nobody need weep at this situation. But for the first time mankind has nowhere on earth to go that he doesn't already know about. We must look the truth in the face, seeing in the world's great mirror exactly what is there and what the earth truly is. In a way this is quite wonderful. We no longer cower in caves; it is the rest of animate creation that flees as we pursue. This is our home. We know all the rooms. We have at least a nodding acquaintance with all the other occupants. But we are the star boarders. Above all, nothing human is alien to us any more. We can't go anywhere else, for all our traveling. We can't meet any different people, for all our seeking. Nobody carries his head under his arm—it's gone out of style.

Not only have the remote regions of the earth (from the Western point of view) been explored and investigated; the empty quarters in our minds have also been filled in. When I was a small boy we used to try to imagine how it would feel to go feet first down a hole through the center of the earth and come out on the other side. We would emerge in China, we thought, upside down. Likewise, we conceived that the Chinese, who were not then the avowed disciples of Karl Marx but rather of Confucius, would be upside down in their ways of life.

But today's Chinese, with a new philosophy overlaid on an old one, like a sweet and sour sauce, still baffle us. Their professed contemporary doctrine is not picturesque or fanciful; it is an unfortunate fact of life with which we have to deal, and it is not amusing. But we cannot evade it, as we evaded so much of what went on in nineteenth century China. The earth is now too small. We can no longer set forth into the brave unknown. We cannot escape anywhere or anybody; the peoples of the earth, in groupings large and small, act and react on each other, and will surely continue doing so. This is one key to the future. It is a door we must unlock.

What travel agent can sell you today the shadow and light of mystery? What Queen can enable you to find these by selling her jewels to pay for your expedition?

4.

We of the Western world have been in the habit of paying calls on foreigners more frequently than they have been willing or able to visit us. The British started this practice in the eighteenth century, when they invented what they called the "Grand Tour." This was an exploit reserved for those Alexander Hamilton called "the rich and well-born." The Grand Tour took in some of the German principalities, as Boswell's pilgrimage did, and it always included France and Italy.

After the Grand Tour had been in operation for about a century, an Englishman invented a plan to send parties hither and yon with pre-arranged reservations. Thus, in

1851, the firm of Thomas Cook was born. The traveler by that time could take a steamer or a railroad, and not have to bring his own carriage and servants with him and hire relays of horses to haul it.

I don't believe the Far East or the heart of Africa ever invented anything like this. The Moslem pilgrimages to Mecca or the Hindu processionals to Benares can hardly be called tourism. Occasionally, of course, well-to-do individuals from the Eastern countries did visit the United States or Britain. East Indian potentates paid calls on Queen Victoria. Sometimes delegates came, their expenses paid by their home Governments.

In our own country Chinese students began to show up early in the present century; the United States used money from the Boxer indemnities, paid by China after the uprisings of 1900, to finance Chinese scholarships here. But this was not tourism, any more than the massive flow of European immigration into this country was such. Actual foreign tourists here have been few in number. Except for the British and ourselves, few nations have produced that peculiar creature who travels around the world merely to gather information and have a good time.

Still, I imagine that if and when world living conditions rise far enough in the now underdeveloped countries, more and more of their people will be able to travel and look us over. I can imagine a group visiting the Capitol at Washington, behind a guide who will speak to them in their native Hindustani, Chinese, Japanese, Swahili, or Arabic.

These people will not come with inflated notions of our modesty and other-worldliness, but they will find us, by their own standards, quaint. They will encounter many features of our lives, including modern plumbing, that they will wish they had more conveniently at home. They may not admire our social culture but they will crave our technological facilities.

This will be, I suspect, a ticklish stage in human history. They will find it hard to understand why life should be so easy in Boston, Massachusetts, and so hard in Recife or Katmandu. You and I can never enter into the mind of a Hindu, an Indonesian, or even a Filipino speaking our own English.

But we are inexorably driven to come closer together, in friendship or otherwise. What we complacently allow other people to call the Americanization of the earth is not that at all: it is the modernization of the earth, the application of known and constantly improving methods to the problems of living. We got hold of these methods because we had a new country and room in which to experiment, not because we were a super-race. With our various tribal and racial strains we were a sort of newer and freer Europe. But the whole Western world is following closely in our trail (in some respects it is ahead of us) and without doubt Africa and the Orient will be along in due season. If the curious and picturesque ways of these regions are too cumbersome, they will be given up—a phenomenon one might call technological determinism.

In Japan and in the Philippines this is already happening; there are evidences of it in Nepal and in the Sudan. Who wants to plow with a water buffalo? Who wants to pile teak with an elephant? Not if a tractor or a diesel engine is available. Who wants to carry water in a bucket or tread a watermill if he has a machine at hand?

5.

We are not inherently superior to other nationalities—or inferior to them, either. If we are as humble as we all ought to be (and had better be), if we can forget the days when we actually were superior in the crude measurement of military strength, we will have much to learn from our outlying and recently dependent neighbors on this earth. The intimate meeting of the cultures should be a creative episode, as was the contact of the West with the old Byzantine learning, when in 1453 the ancient capital on the Bosphorus fell to the Turks.

What followed this event was called the Renaissance. This might have occurred even if so many learned men had not felt it prudent to settle in Italy. But there was a sharp contact between old and new. Eastern and Western culture intermingled and a great upheaval came out of it. The discovery of America came out of it.

Something like this encounter of East and West might happen again—maybe is happening. The East might give a new appraisal to what has been going on for the past few centuries in the West. Now that the imperialism of power is about over, there may be a weakening of the imperialism of culture.

We find Japanese movies interesting. African and Oriental rhythms get into our music and our dances; their arts into our design. The quietism of the East might weaken the Western belief that almost any expenditure of energy is good. And of course we might remind the East that doing something for oneself is often helpful for others and that we may not have been put into the world merely to contemplate our navels.

This sort of process cannot take place all at once. Nothing important, except death and destruction, happens all at once. What is certain is that the fractions of humanity, once scattered widely, are beginning to add up into a new equation. Like it or not, we shall henceforth influence one another more and more—if only in a further refinement and perfection of the means of killing one another.

The native girls do not swim out around the ships any more, but the copra trade is organized; it yields soap, cosmetics, drugs, chemicals, and things to eat. That man down the beach is not Gauguin, but he is a real live painter and is arranging for a one-man show on Fifty-seventh Street this fall.

The South Seas may now attract few romantic writers. There aren't many such, anyhow. Some new Dreiser or Sinclair Lewis, some new Maugham or Michener may still sweep up dusty remnants of the Second World War or study the debilitating effects of the tourist trade on the natives, but no Melville, no Robert Louis Stevenson.

I have lost the name of the author, an Englishman who had grow tired of England, and who wrote sorrowfully from some mid-Pacific shore that when he had got twelve thousand miles from home he could get no farther; every foot of travel after that would bring him nearer the beloved and detested place where he was born.

We shall, of course, continue in motion, but the motion will henceforth be more in the nature of a swirl—the constant, almost invisible dance of particles in a liquid that physicists call the Brownian movement.

We can now go farther faster than ever before in human

experience—and this acceleration seems to be only begin-ning. We are also able to see less and learn less in less time—a great saving of something, I forget what.

Let us, in the next chapter, take a look at this strange phenomenon.

VI

•••••••

Motion:
The Modern Neurosis

MAN HAS ALWAYS been, when he could be, a traveling animal. True, he was often hedged in, as he was in American Indian days, by unfriendly neighbors who wanted no alien fishing or hunting on their tribal lands. The primitive Indians of California, for instance, could not travel more than a few miles without getting into a new dialect area and lots of trouble. Ancient language barriers in Africa often ran parallel with the coast, whereas European intrusion, when it came, was naturally inland from the beach. Under such circumstances people either stayed home or undertook wars of conquest. The tourist business didn't flourish.

But when men could travel, anywhere on earth, they generally did. The South Sea Islanders hopped gaily from island to island, in what should have been, but generally weren't, unseaworthy canoes. Most people think they went in an easterly or a southeasterly direction, others prefer to believe they originated in South or Central America and went westward. It doesn't matter too much; they went.

They went where the cruise ships and the airplanes go today, only more slowly. They desired to know what lay beyond the horizon. They wanted room for more people, so they would not have to drown so many girl babies. And somehow the wandering instinct got into the blood; they went because they wanted to go; they were tired of old camping places and cold ashes.

The wandering instinct may have been, in fact, an element of survival; races and tribes that had this instinct had a better chance of being fruitful and multiplying than those that didn't. Whether the human race grew up in one center or in several centers simultaneously, its perpetuation—and pretty dubious this was during the first few thousand years—depended on its spreading; it had to make use of all the friendly or supportable environments it could reach before some other form of life came along and put up signs saying keep out—strictly private—trespassers will be prosecuted—this means you. And like the bedbug in the old proverb, they did get there.

When our remote ancestors stopped being arboreal they tended to be pastoral. They domesticated animals, milked them, rode on them, ate them, used their skins. In some areas of the world—for example, in Norway, Scotland, parts of Africa, Mongolia—the pastures were better in the lowlands at certain seasons and in the highlands at other seasons. The animals themselves, such as the American bison, migrated to and fro, and the hunters, knowing their habits, followed them. Those who have read (and maybe re-read) Parkman's *Oregon Trail* may recall that Parkman had quite a time getting in touch with a migratory Sioux "village" when he wished to study Indians in their native habitat. A Sioux village was in fact a hunting range, never a long-settled community.

In the same way migratory hunters the world over had to move their camps from time to time as the game drifted. Sometimes they seem to have made these excursions from a fixed base, but on other occasions, like the Sioux, they took the whole community along. The young men also went on the war path when life at home became meagre or dull.

Until man began to be numerous, he had plenty of room in which to move around, and the moving was good for him. So the human race has an instinct to move about and usually still finds it fun; the travelers who swarm off the planes or cruise ships at ports of call are spiritual descendants of Attila's wild warriors, Marco Polo's horse-wranglers, and Columbus' jailbirds.

If we read our history carefully, we also find that some communities have moved not for fun, but because other communities were pressing in on them. The plains of central Eurasia, from the Pacific to the Baltic and North Sea, to the Atlantic and Mediterranean, seem to have been swept repeatedly by masses of westward-driving people, some of them in flight from enemies, or perhaps driven by drought or other forms of bad weather. Thus the Visigoths and the Ostrogoths came into the Roman Empire and destroyed it, and in a smaller migration of peoples, the Angles, Saxons, and Jutes entered Britain and much later were taken in hand by the invading Normans. Cornwall, Wales, and the highlands of Scotland were peopled by tribes of Celtic derivation who pushed in or were chased in from somewhere else.

These migrations may not always have been enjoyable,

but there must have been thrills in all of them. How and why did the Finns occupy Finland? Their language has a cousinship with the Hungarian or Magyar. Earlier inhabitants of Finland, the Lapps, were pushed northward—as is usual in such cases, off the best land.

What made the Norsemen for a long time so formidable? Anybody who has ever made an excursion along a Norwegian fjord will know why they wanted to get away— also, why they loved to come home again.

Why do so many persons today like to go hunting, camping, back-packing, fishing, canoeing, horseback riding? Why are there gold rushes, diamond rushes, uranium rushes? Surely it is because we have an aversion, in many cases, to settling down. We like to get rich, too, but that is another matter, another madness. Any healthy young man would rather find a solid gold boulder up in the foothills somewhere (this has happened in California, and maybe elsewhere) than sit with his feet up while his stock doubles or triples in value.

There are exceptions to all generalizations—even this one. My wife and I once knew a family in the Basque lands of France, who had lived on the same lands for seven hundred years. They had grown to like the place, though as they multiplied, individual members had had to go away to make a living. There must have been many such families. And I was once told of a philosophical citizen in Weston, Connecticut, who boasted that he had never been to New York City, fifty miles away. We know now that Thoreau did much far traveling in Concord—he said this himself.

But most of us like to go far, and when we can we do. And some of us don't find it too hard to migrate, Modern

America boils and churns like a pot of mush on a hot stove.

2.

The United States was, of course, mainly populated by immigrants, from the Spaniards and Puritans down, though the natural increase by birth has also been large. Nor must we forget the Indians who were already here, not great in numbers, but important. The late Frederick Jackson Turner based his entire theory of American history on the influence of the frontier, the westward movement, the git-up-and-git impulse.

How dear to our hearts is the old covered wagon! (And how ill-used we would feel if we had to cross the continent in one.) Rolling over the National Road from Philadelphia to Pittsburgh, wallowing through the mountains on the old Wilderness Trail into Kentucky, bumping and swaying into Missouri, and along the Sante Fe, Oregon, and California trails and their countless branches, across the fords of the Platte and the Arkansas; down the rugged headlands of the Columbia Valley; over the Sierras by Donner Lake into somewhat Golden California—these are memories that will never die. There was space then, and great hardship and danger, and no overcrowding except sometimes around the water holes.

Nor will the legends of the great rivers perish: keel boats plunging down the headwaters of the Tennessee and the Cumberland, and down the Ohio into the Mississippi; rafts on the Mississippi and the sleek side-wheel steamers of which Mark Twain was the pilot and unforgettable reporter; military expeditions up the headwaters of the Missouri, into the Yellowstone River, Maria's River; steamboats whistling mournfully up and down the Sacramento River before the railroad and the motor car took their livelihood away—these remain ours, these are American, this was the way we settled the country when there was still plenty of land, plenty of malaria, plenty of wood to cut or buffalo chips to burn, plenty of wild game. And nobody who had youth and muscle had to take any back talk from anybody; he could pack a horse, a mule, or a burro and get the hell out of there. Sometimes it really was hell; but it was motion, it was change.

The frontiersmen, as delineated by such finicky observers as Parkman, did not smell good and sometimes had uncouth manners; they drank too much, but there they were—as good as anyone and maybe better.

They moved. They moved about as fast as the Roman had done two thousand years earlier, though their roads were not as good as the Roman highways. Riders with relays of horses did as much as a hundred miles a day; the Pony Express briefly carried the mail at ten miles an hour on level ground; stage coaches across the Plains in good weather did almost as well. But these were stunts. The frontiersman also went on foot to impossible places, expertly concealing the traces of his camps if he were in the land of hostile Indians.

I think these men loved it. Their narratives, even in the midst of dire privation, suggest as much. There was a difference, of course, between the free life of the trapper and that of the pioneer who had his wife and children, perhaps his plow, with him. But even Francis Parkman, a careful historian if there ever was one, but no poet, wrote of the exaltation he and his companion felt as they rode along the base of the mountains at the foot of Pike's Peak. Parkman would go back to Boston weakened by the ravages of digestive diseases acquired among the Indians, but I am sure he often dreamed of the wild freedom and the utterly un-Bostonian joy of the sparsely peopled Great Plains.

Not many decades after, the railroads bestrode the prairies, plains, Rocky Mountains, and Sierras, and about a generation and a half after that the automobile arrived. The old exhilaration of totally untouched country would come no more; what had taken thousands of years in Europe, the taming of a continent, needed only a few swift lifetimes in America.

3.

The automobile arrived almost imperceptibly. At first, the common people hated it because they thought it a rich man's toy. They told the rich, in no uncertain terms, to go get a horse. The rich ignored this churlish advice. Instead, the poor, to their great surprise, found that they too needed and could get automobiles. As I leaf through the *World Almanac* I find that 4,192 motor vehicles were sold in 1900. Total registration in 1966 was well above eighty-two million—and will doubtless increase unless driving a car is found to cause cancer of the right foot. This is one motor vehicle for each two and a fraction Americans, babes in arms included.

Since I am, after all, trying to be a prophet rather than a historian (which is easier, because by the time you are found out you are dead) I shall not play around with statistics. Except when we are up in the air we are a nation on wheels. Insofar as our towns and cities are being planned at all, which isn't always, they are patterned for a population that would rather go hungry than stop driving.

The word explosion comes to mind again and again. The universe is possibly exploding, though I hope not. Human population is certainly exploding. Our cities are exploding, and not only American cities but cities the whole world over. Find me a city and I will show you a rush to it. Not even Moscow and Peking, those centers of boastfully planned societies, are immune to this symptom or disease—whichever it is. When people can get to a city they generally do. And it *is* a rush.

Not just a rush hour, but a rush year, a rush generation: that is the story. But the motor car is producing a totally different type of city to rush to. People don't like to drive downtown into the congested areas to shop. Therefore, all across the United States, and in other countries as well, there has been a mushrooming of peripheral shopping "centers"—the humor in this designation is that their great advantage is that they are not "central" at all.

This is true of San Francisco and of a small Western city where I happen to be living; it is true of Washington, D. C., and of New York City; it is true of Rome, Italy, and I have read of a plan to manufacture "another Paris" outside the existing French city of that name. Downtown Paris, I take it, is to remain a reservation for tourists and for the business ventures that cater to—or prey upon—tourists.

In theory the automobile is a flexible device for transportation; in practice, in large cities and on congested highways, it is about as flexible as a freight car; it will not take you conveniently where you want to go, for too many other automobiles will be in the way.

On the other hand, the train is not flexible, either. It is tied to schedules, tracks, and stations. It is an efficient machine for one purpose alone: carrying large numbers of people from one fixed point to another fixed point. Usually it cannot carry an individual from where he lives to where he works. He has to reach the station, formerly by street car or even by walking, now by taxi, bus, or private car; at the end of his trip he has to take a bus, a subway, or a taxi to his workaday destination.

It is a rather alarming symptom that in recent years, in many surburban areas, local buses have tended to disappear. The inter-urban, long-distance bus has meanwhile multiplied and has increased its range. It does not seem to me as comfortable as an old-style upholstered passenger coach, but its stations are usually nearer the center of town than the railway stations. That is, if the towns have any real centers any more.

The results are curious. Branch railroads have almost disappeared—fewer passengers, not enough paying freight, too much truck competition. Some railroads would like to get rid of all short-run traffic, even on their main lines. This is because short-line business is falling off. On the other hand, short-line business is falling off because the short-run trains are fewer, less convenient, and less comfortable. They don't have to be that way; they are often almost deliberately made so. As one who has loved railroads and railroading for half a century or so, I say this regretfully. I wouldn't bring the stage coach back, even if I could, but I do recall sadly some beautiful trains I have ridden on.

Another difficulty for railroads is that they have to build and maintain their own tracks. Bus companies pay taxes of various kinds, including a tax intended to keep up the highways but often diverted to other uses. But when a stretch of road deteriorates we do not expect the bus companies, all by themselves, to renovate it; we build a freeway, throughway, or speedway, at enormous expense, and tax or bond everybody above the age of twenty-one to pay the bill.

If we really wished to transport great numbers of people, on the surface and at high speeds, we would invent or reinvent the railroad. In spite of a few tentative experiments we do not do this, because the automobile companies carry much weight in our economy, and in spite of the regimentation we read about, the typical citizen likes to have his own private transportation in his own garage; he likes to start when he wants to, go the way he wants to, and park close to his base of operations. His wife, if he is well enough heeled to have two cars, will take the children to school in her own vehicle, go shopping and carry on her daily social life by car. If he and his wife can afford only one car, she drives him to the station. This is the pattern of surburban living. The automobile makes us more and more suburban.

I returned a year or so ago to a small city I had lived in as a young man. It had been a small town in those days, with many green spaces. Now this city has a lovely wild-life park, up in the hills back yonder with many green spaces, but such of the once open downtown spaces as remain are mostly filled, at busy hours, with parked cars. So are the outlying portions of the Campus of the nearby university.

These parking places and the ranks of cars they contain are convenient but not beautiful. I think we may make better arrangements bye and bye. This kind of ugliness isn't worthwhile. Someday we may come to think of beauty in our surroundings as one of the necessities of life.

For some years, as part of a journalistic life, I watched the efforts of Manhattan Island to adapt itself to the motor age. During this period the time required to drive at legal speeds from Washington Square to certain points in Fairfield County, Connecticut, diminished by at least an hour; we didn't have to use the antiquated Boston Post Road any more. But there was one condition attached to this quick and easy driving; other people soon learned about it, as they always do, and you had to drive on odd days at odd hours to escape the long jams that developed. Too much convenience, in short, made driving inconvenient.

The city of New York, indeed, made it fantastically easy to drive into Manhattan and fantastically hard to find a good place to park after you arrived. Cars flowed in like water into a reservoir (and for cars there was never a drought) and in no time at all the reservoir was filled. And as service by private cars and by buses improved, service by railroad was allowed to deteriorate.

This was true all around the New York area. Later I noticed similar conditions centering upon the much smaller city of San Francisco, and heard so much about the Los Angeles region that I was afraid to go down there to find out for myself.

If these situations continue long enough our great cities will smother to death. We need a miracle.

4.

A traffic specialist once told me what he considered to be the optimum speed needed to get the most cars past a given point on a given road in a given time. It was not sixty, or seventy, or a hundred miles an hour; for when you are planning traffic movements you wish to have drivers and passengers alive and whole at the end of the run and must therefore allow for increased distances between cars at increased speeds. The best speed, as I recall, was thirty-five miles an hour. Better brakes may have enabled us to raise this figure—but not, I am persuaded, very much. You can't move traffic at a uniform high speed per hour unless you hitch it together like a railroad train.

The modern passenger automobile may until very recently have lacked some safety factors, but it is a wonderful machine (the advertisements do not conceal this fact). It is, however, designed and powered to travel more than thirty-five miles an hour. There are parkways and freeways, turnpikes and express highways, coast to coast, where a mile a minute is not only possible but is accepted as a legal and even praiseworthy speed. These high speeds do not save time when a large number of drivers wish to go the same way in the same space at the same hour. But when possible they are fun.

The automobile manufacturers no longer advertise speed as vociferously as they used to; they treat it as a safety factor, for with a reserve of horsepower you can pass another car more safely, although there may be no need of passing it at all—or any sense in it. And cars are still named by titles suggesting swift movement; read a flock of motor car advertisements and see for yourself. Some drivers jump at any chance to speed: they love velocity like a drug.

Yet my own amazement as I read today's statistics of sales and registrations is not that quite a few persons are killed or wounded in an average year, but that so many who drive stay alive and healthy. The human race in the Western world has accustomed itself to fairly frightful speeds and the resulting dangers. Perhaps the racial strains that can adapt themselves to high speed and that have a swift reaction time will survive. I don't suppose the motor car will kill us off any more than the various ice ages and pestilences have; it is more like a wild animal in the jungle that you can avoid if you are careful.

Of course we have to relate speed to its usefulness. We have to distinguish between the speed that will get a physician to his patient quickly or a fireman to his fire, and the other kind of speed, which seems to make a driver feel good and forget his troubles. The great highways serve both purposes: convenience and hell-raising. The convenience is convenient, but I do believe the hell-raising will sooner or later have to be taken severely in hand.

It might be a good plan to have special highways for especially reckless people, leaving other highways for mild-mannered persons who merely want to go somewhere, and who do not have to prove their manliness by endangering their own and other lives. The reckless would kill one another, which would not be a shattering loss to anybody but their loved ones; the non-reckless would tend to stay alive and die later of the customary ailments of old age.

Another thought comes to me, though I do not know that this proposal is right, or even legal. This is that the devil-may-care type of drivers, full of beans, arrogance, and sometimes alcohol, be extracted from their cars and given, free of charge, perhaps by a sub-division of Medicare, a drug that would make them *think* they were rushing wildly through space, passing all other vehicles and overtaking stray comets.

I am not in favor of prohibiting motor cars. I merely suggest we make wiser use of the great good that is in them. The motor car, as we have recently been reminded, has its drawbacks as well as its uses; but as a formerly young man who once had to curry, feed, water, and hitch up a horse before going on a milk route, I hope it will not disappear. Let us, perhaps somewhat chastened, include it in our future commonwealth, our mechanical pseudo-utopia.

The time may come (though this hardly seems likely today) when we will not have to go anywhere. All our work will be done in our own homes by pressing buttons, pulling small levers, and telephoning. There may not be anywhere to go—everywhere may be full of people wishing they were somewhere else but unable because of the congestion to get there. Until then we will have to have automotive vehicles, though not necessarily a new model every fall.

I imagine we may put restrictions on motor cars in cities, just as we do on pigs and other domestic animals running at large. This won't bankrupt Detroit. It will merely make it more fun to drive a motor car in suitable places.

5.

Passenger airplanes are, of course, another form of the motion neurosis. The air may even become crowded. My

own memory goes back to the time when if an airplane got
off the ground this was a miracle. (It was.) Bleriot flew the
English Channel, straddling an over-heated engine that
scorched his legs; Glenn Curtiss, in 1910, flew from Manhattan to Albany and back; Lindbergh made his famous
non-stop flight from New York to Paris in 1927, carrying a
letter of introduction in case the French immigration
officials should wonder who he was! But there were no
commerical passenger flights across the Atlantic or the
Pacific until after the Second World War.

Commercial use of the airplane would have come eventually, for anything that is worth money, and some things
that are not, can be sold. But military flying in both great
wars stimulated the progress of flying. In the end it became
commonplace for a traveler to cross the Atlantic in a fraction of the time Lindbergh required in his lumbering *Spirit
of St. Louis.*

Millions of us have now flown the Atlantic and other
oceans, more bored than adventurous, and delighted (some
of them, not sulky bookworms or scenery mongers like
myself) with the prospect of seeing a new movie on the
way. For such there are no ticker-tape parades, nor for the
pilots and crew, either.

The airplane is extraordinarily convenient, once you get
where it is. The helicopter simplifies the journey to the
airfield—all you have to do then is to get to where the helicopter is. At any rate, increasing numbers of us find ourselves in the big jet planes, some of which could put the
first Wright brothers' "kites" in their baggage compartments. The jet planes, as I write, do six or seven hundred
miles an hour—the equivalent of about forty days in a
covered wagon crossing the Great Plains. It is not con-

sidered fast enough, however. Why, when time is so precious, waste five and a half hours going from New York to a Pacific Coast city? Airplanes have been flown at two thousand miles an hour, and we are promised this speed in commercial service by 1972.

We can go two thousand miles an hour on all long-distance runs if we are willing to pay for it. Let us consider what happens then. The difference in standard time between New York and San Francisco is three hours. When it is twelve o'clock noon in New York it is only nine in the morning in San Francisco. A traveler leaving New York at noon can therefore arrive at the San Francisco airport at about half-past ten, local time. Despite the customary ground congestion the passenger will be able to get to his hotel in downtown San Francisco at a little after eleven—almost an hour earlier in terms of local time than when he left New York.

This is an astounding achievement. Even Joshua could only make the sun stand still; our traveler from the Atlantic seaboard has actually pushed the sun backward. But we all know what will happen. Our bird of passage, who is, for example, a big toothbrush manufacturer, will do some telephoning, maybe about toothbrushes and maybe not. Then he will have lunch with a business friend. He will have at least two cocktails to precede it, and he and his friend will spend at least half the next three hours discussing mutual acquaintances, baseball, or politics before they get down to the big deal that really brought him to town.

It strikes me that the speed urge in this case is childish. It is the more so because, at the now customary high flight altitudes, one has very little sense of speed. One gets to places, especially at night or above fog and clouds, without having been anywhere. One leaves Washington, say, or Boston or New York, has a drink, eats something, reads a newspaper, possibly—God forbid!—looks at That Movie; then glances out the window and sees that one is letting down for San Francisco; that corrugated plain below, if the weather happens to be clear, is either the Rocky Mountains or the Sierras—in these days it hardly matters which.

The luxury of distance has vanished. Your sense of enormous speed comes only when the plane taxis off and when it comes down; at such times you are aware that you are riding the fastest automobile on earth.

I have tried and tried to make sense out of the continued efforts to produce ever greater velocities. I cannot help feeling that the investors, the inventors, and the engineers who are working so hard in the extra-supersonic field are rational in ways I cannot grasp. I may add that as a passenger I am not a Johnny-come-lately in this area—I took my first plane ride nearly half a century ago. But I cannot help feeling that sixty times what was good enough for—I won't say for Moses, because he had a chariot of fire—but for George Washington, Abraham Lincoln, or John Greenleaf Whittier is good enough for me. How can I stand to stay in one spot for as long as six seconds? Why don't I get a horse?

6.

The truth is that the earth would now be almost as small as the state of Rhode Island or even that romantic gambling house that is called the principality of Monaco if it were not for two factors: money and politics. Unless some military advantage is conceived, we cannot afford mass migrations by air. The peasant in India or in the communist anthills in China could not afford to pay his own fare to Omaha. The tourist from the developed (or even overdeveloped) countries goes increasingly about the globe, now that his income is so large and his curiosity so great. He is penetrating those parts of the Far East and Africa that are not, at the moment, undergoing a revolution, whose inhabitants do not hate white people with money in their jeans and who have diplomatic relations with the United States and other respectable nations.

The old International Set—the new Jet Set—that used to do the round of capitals and watering places in Europe, still exists, I am told, but goes to farther places.

Tourist excursions (naturally of a less glittering order) do not, as far as can be ascertained, cause interbreeding among the Western and Eastern tribes. Yet the two kinds of culture—ours and theirs, Western and Eastern—do come into closer contact than ever before. It is no longer a case of an American ship with beaver and other furs dropping into the harbor of Canton or Hong Kong. It is quite a stream of foreigners from the West who want to see the natives while the natives are still cute.

The natives are getting less cute every day. The Koreans, north and south, are no longer funny little men with queer, conical hats; the mainland Chinese are not now in our eyes picturesque specimens who cannot pronounce the letter "r" and who carry burdens slung on the ends of poles across their shoulders; the East Indians are divided now into two distinct countries, whose inhabitants, for religious motives, often have an impulse to kill people on the other side of the boundary line; the Indonesians no longer suggest merely coffee, spices, and a gastronomic indiscretion called the "rice table"; South Africa does not recall Cecil Rhodes and the Cape of Good Hope—it is now the symbol for an anachronistic, terrible, and unhopeful racial predicament.

We travel more seriously now, perhaps less joyously, possibly with less arrogance and pretence; we are now being judged while we judge, and we know it. Passengers from the cruise ships, who love to travel with less than the speed of sound, go about the earth in droves and clutches, buying native products made by German or Japanese factories, taking pictures, but sometimes slightly troubled and uncertain. For in this new dispensation every city is a suburb of some other city, the world around.

The whole sea of humanity, wherever it has gathered on the earth's surface, is being stirred around by destiny's mighty egg-beater. Nothing and nobody will ever seem as strange to us as they did to our parents; the Taj Mahal and the Pyramids, the Acropolis and the brooding statues on Easter Island are just around the corner now. No Argonauts, in a thunder and wonder of colors, will ever seek the Golden Fleece again.

A sobering thought is that the peoples of the less fortunate areas of the earth will soon know that there is no magic about us, either; they will soon know, if they do not know at present, how luxuriously we of the more fortunate areas live. We shall all see more of one another than we used to do in the dear dead days of long ago. We may even feel remorse that these, our brothers, are so neglected.

We have plenty of apples in our part of the world, and

plenty of peanuts. It may not be enough, once the truth is spread about as we go traveling, merely to hand out the cores and shucks to the needy in other lands. If democracy is to gain and survive anywhere, it can have no fences around it. There will have to be democracy among the nations as well as among individuals—not a patent medicine or other nostrum but an actual equality of rights that enables men to respect themselves and one another.

We are milling about the earth like ants in an overturned anthill, bees in a swarming nest, migrating birds that winter in the Arctic and summer in Patagonia; never at rest any more, never satisfied to be where we are, intoxicated by the drugs of distance and soothed by the anodyne of speed.

This outcome was not planned or even anticipated by anybody. It just happened, and now it cannot unhappen. As I try to put together what the newspapers, magazines, books, radio, and television tell us of what is going on around the world I feel the mighty rush of history accelerating past my ears.

VII

Moon Madness

A MAN I KNEW used to argue with me because I was sceptical about the value of moon shots and such. If I had been born in the reign of Ferdinand and Isabella or in the age of England's first Elizabeth, he said, I would have been equally hard to convince of the value of crossing oceans and civilizing the heathen who were perhaps on the other side of the water.

My rejoinder was that the late medieval and early modern explorations were measurably profitable to those who paid for them and made them; they uncovered real estate that could often be had for nothing down and nothing a month; they revealed stores of gold that the explorers and conquistadores regarded as honest plunder; they brought millions of cheap and usually submissive workers into the international labor market; and they promoted trade; the West could send furs to China in exchange for tea and silk, or bring slaves from Africa to the West Indies and some American states in exchange for rum.

This made sense, in terms of the pertinent dates. It makes sense even today, although the march of progress has raised the prices both of labor and of goods from such regions as the Indies and the west coast of Africa.

No doubt there was also satisfaction for the great captains—Columbus, Magellan, Drake, and the rest—merely in finding the unknown. But curiosity was never enough to raise the needed money. Ferdinand and Isabella, Elizabeth and James, wanted something they could take to the grocery store to pay for what they ate. Nothing gave a sixteenth- or seventeenth-century monarch more concern for the souls of the heathen than hope of such fringe benefits as gold and fertile land. The easy money did not begin to peter out until the American colonies revolted and cut their enforced commercial and political relations with Britain. The mother countries in all cases aspired to sell manufactured goods in their colonies at high prices and buy raw materials in a cheap market. This was a good racket for the manufacturers, while it lasted.

I was able to point out these considerations to my enthusiastic friend. There are no natives on the moon to be converted or exploited. I further inquired as to what he supposed we would find on the moon or any accessible planet that would pay the costs of space travel? We all have to pay tribute to the skill and courage of the so-designated astronauts (a poor term, for they do not deal with stars) and to the incredible refinements of devices that have enabled them to circumnavigate the earth in a few hours or days, over and over again. I told him I knew about this, for I had read the advertisements of those who sold the government the ingredients needed for space ships, and they all spoke well of themselves. Magellan's men saw more because they were on the surface, but it took those of them who survived three tough years to make the trip.

Exploring the earth was worthwhile in many ways. There remains doubt as to whether the game of moon-bumping or planet-tickling is worth the cost of the rockets it will take. It is diverting, of course, but is it diverting enough for the billions of dollars it costs?

My friend hinted vaguely (he was getting groggy by this time) that there might be precious metals on the moon—not necessarily gold or uranium, but metals useful to industry. He did not contend that this could be true of Venus or Mars, much less Saturn or Mercury. I asked if such metals or minerals would be worth the money they cost and the risk of life required to get them. He said many men died on the voyages of Columbus and Magellan. I said, why couldn't we simulate moon conditions in some desert down here and have just as much fun, including risk of life, at less expense.

I then went home and continued to read about the subject. I wanted to change my mind and agree with my neighbors, but couldn't. I learned that the atmosphere of Venus is probably too hot to be penetrated, though there may be bearably cool spots at the poles. I found out that Mars is not and has not been inhabited by anybody as large and bumptious as a human being, and may not even contain a self-respecting microbe. We have learned something about the geography of the moon, including that of the far side, but there is still some concern as to whether anybody who lands there will ever be able to get off his rocket ship, even though he wears rubber boots and snow shoes and has a credit card.

It may be that somebody—or some team—will devise a

sort of moon-scooter that will enable explorers on the moon to tear around and learn things. This scooter will have to be completely enclosed, and perhaps it will have hot and cold running water, steam heat, and a kitchen in which the wanderer can eat prepared flapjacks with maple syrup. I have boundless faith in human ingenuity. But the price of the ticket?

2.

Is it worthwhile to a baseball team to win the World Series? Does an invitation to the Rose Bowl, the Sugar Bowl, or the Chopping Bowl prove that Siwash College has a better team than the football specialists from Nowash University?

Competitively, in moon shots as well as in baseball and football, there is satisfaction for the winner. And the competitive spirit is of value for human progress. Let us suppose we land one man on the moon. The Russians will reply by landing two men on the moon—bigger ones than ours, of course; the Chinese, if they can, will then land three men. Each set of explorers will bring back samples of the lunar surface. Each will explain on radio, on television, and in print, how it feels to be on the moon. Each will have a ticker-tape parade, up Broadway, across the Red Square, or through what used to be the Forbidden City.

Much interesting information will be brought back by each expedition, though perhaps not more than could be obtained through the use of instruments. The moon may also have military uses. Possibly the nation that gets there first may lawfully claim it; it will then be an American, Russian, or Chinese moon, though it looks almost the same as before. It might become the fifty-first American state, and send one Representative and two Senators to Washington.

As a military object—a sort of Gilraltar in the sky—it might enable the garrison to direct projectiles with more accuracy than is now possible. But the military advantages of using the moon as an offensive satellite do not seem to me, as I read or hear about them, worth the bother of establishing bases there.

We may, of course ("we" meaning America in this case), join with other nations in exploring and perhaps developing the moon. President Kennedy offered to cooperate with the Russians in this venture, and President Johnson has renewed the offer.

The moon can be a source of useful information. It cannot be a place to colonize or exploit; for such a purpose the Antarctic Continent would be by contrast pleasant and pastoral. Let us not cherish illusions. The moon is not much good, except to take bearings on, to make tides and to stimulate romance.

Nor, according to what we are told, is Venus or Mars. If Venus is not too hot and Mars is not too mushy, I do not question that man can land on both planets. But what good would such an inter-planetary exploit, a Solar System World Series, do? I am as curious as anybody, but I cannot think of any information or advantage from such exploits that would be worth the bother. I can hardly believe that inter-planetary exploring will have much to do with humanity's future.

I shall continue to read science fiction on the rare occasions when I feel like it; but as likely as not I shall pick up

Jules Verne or H. G. Wells before I risk losing myself in the dizzy intricacies of modern space travel. I suggest, let the romancers wash their own flying saucers.

3.

If we don't go to far-out places in the universe, I hear it said, can't we at least try to communicate with them? I imagine the answer is no, we can't.

David, the Psalmist wrote, in words made beautiful in the King James Version: "When I consider Thy heavens, the work of Thy fingers, the moon and the stars which Thou hast ordained, what is man that Thou art mindful of him?" David had been a shepherd and had seen the firmament at night. Today's astronomers have more facts than he did, but this merely leads them to argue whether this is a "steady state" universe, an expanding universe, or a pulsating universe—and whether, if it does pulsate, it does this all at once in all places or occasionally and only in some places. But the facts have not changed much since David's time. This is not a universe we can ever explore. It is not a sociable universe. As a whole it does not seem to know man is alive.

Let us now consider the matter of communication with possible worlds we cannot conceivably visit. We are now able to pick up any messages that come through, with or without commercials. No recognizable message has yet arrived—but who knows? One may.

We have listening stations. Listening at one of these is a dull life, unless one is keenly interested in static. However, something could come through that would indicate the existence of highly intelligent beings elsewhere. A mathematical formula might be the universal language—and "universal" in such a case would have an enlarged meaning. Two and two apparently everywhere, no matter how far away, would equal four. Some form of the famous Einstein equation, indicating the enormous energy locked up in the atom, might come out of space; I can't see how, but there are those who can. And there is always the chance that those people out there might be a good deal brighter than we are, which would be both helpful and humiliating.

But what does the possibility of even the most successful communication with planets in other star systems come down to? The nearest such system that may have attendant planets conceivably fit to support intelligent life, is 4.3 light years away. Light moves at the rate of 186,000 miles a second, and a light year is thus the equivalent of 186,000 times 60, times 60, times 24, times 365.25—too far to walk.

Other star systems are millions, even billions of light years away; when we are engaged in considering the firmament we do not see a contemporary universe; we are looking into the vast depths of time as well as of space; we may be seeing stars that no longer exist; we speak of stars that seem fixed and related, yet are separated from us and from one another by immeasurable gaps.

A message might come from a being so many light years away that whoever or whatever sent it may have lived in what is now a dead and empty planet. The thought makes a body feel lonesome. It's no use trying to form an inter-stellar club; it would be eternally impossible for any two members to be present at the same time.

We may let our imaginations play, however, on a situation that might occur near Alpha Centauri—the one that is only 4.3 light years away. Anybody living on a planet in that vicinity is likely to overlap some individual life on earth—a great many of such lives, in fact. Suppose, then, that we—or those among us who can do such things—open up communication with a planet in the Alpha Centauri system. This would take time, but let us suppose that finally we are able to transmit not only telegraphic signals but words and pictures in color.

Now we are all set for one of those inter-stellar romances. A young scientist is working in an observatory on top of a Rocky Mountain peak—up Wind River way somewhere. He is unmarried, intelligent, handsome, wholesome, and suffering from unrequited love for a girl in Trenton, New Jersey. He has come out west to forget. His name is Egbert. Almost any girl can get him on the rebound.

Suddenly there flashes on the screen before him, instead of the usual geometric design, a ravishing young female named, as far as he can make out (transliteration between planets will always be difficult), Phoebe. She is not, as he had at first supposed, a soap advertisement that has drifted out of its proper circuit, although she is lovely enough even for that. She has blonde, brown, black, or red hair, whichever he prefers. Her eyes are gray, black, blue, or brown, again whichever he likes. She has a luscious mouth, a pert little nose, a slim and graceful figure with satisfactory chest measurements.

She has a message for him. She has been watching him from afar, like the washer-woman in Gilbert's *Pinafore*, and she loves him. That is, she did love him 4.3 years ago. Will he marry her? (On Phoebe's planet girls save a lot of bother by asking these questions themselves.)

Of course he will marry her, he doesn't know just how; he gets off a message to that effect at once. By the time this reaches her, 8.6 years will have elapsed since she made her proposition. Arrangements for the ceremony will then have to be worked out. Perhaps he will be able to arrange for a space ship that will carry him at the fastest speed known in the universe—that of light. (He will pretend he is interested solely in pure science.) Altogether, I estimate that about eighty years will have elapsed before the impatient lovers can meet and consummate the marriage.

The ending of this particular piece of science fiction will be all the sadder if he arrives for the wedding a decrepit old man of a hundred and one, and finds that in the Alpha Centauri set-up, life has been so successfully prolonged that Phoebe still appears like a blooming maiden of twenty-one, though she is really exactly her lover's age. I pass over the possible biological differences; Phoebe, like Egbert, was made in the supposed image of the Creator. Thus, if Egbert, at his age, is still interested, the two can mate.

There are many variations as to what happens next. Suppose Egbert and Phoebe, despite his advanced age, generate several children on Phoebe's planet. Assume he then wishes to take her to the planet Earth, as he naturally would, to show her and her offspring to the old folks—who by this time are getting far along in years. The space trip, with three children (two lively boys and one rather horrid little girl), will be a rather frustrating experience; the children will want to get out and walk; the parents will be cramped, uncomfortable, and irritable; each will blame the situation on the other.

When the family arrives at the selected earthly spaceport Egbert will be nearly a hundred and ten years old, whereas Phoebe will still seem young and lovely. There will be much newspaper publicity. Undergraduates in universities including Harvard, Yale, Stanford and possibly the University of Chicago, will fall in love with her; she will reciprocate, because in her planet that is all right.

Fiercely jealous, Egbert will sue for divorce. He will win, but because of the unusual circumstances the judge will allow Phoebe (to whom he is, indeed, secretly attracted) custody of the children for half the time. She returns to her own planet but must bring them back to visit Egbert in about nine years. Egbert retires to his den in the Wind River Mountains, but instead of listening to radio broadcasts from space he merely walks around glaring at the firmament and muttering "pfui," or some word like that.

I have not tried to be frivolous in discussing this melancholy series of events. I wish merely to draw attention to the difficulties of communicating with other inhabited worlds, if such there be. I think we have to face the probability that actual visiting among the extra-solar planets will always be limited under the laws of Nature as we know them, and that inter-galaxy conversations, by whatever means, will be pretty awful.

Here we are, I suggest, and here we stay. The universe is no tea party. We will observe most of it forever at a distance, like an astronaut (that misleading word again) glimpsing from one hundred miles or more up a church sociable in Little Tootling, Herefordshire, England.

4.

We are learning a great deal about the universe. And our descendants, if any, will learn much more. Like ourselves, they will have an insatiable curiosity as to what is going on out there. Though they will most likely land on the moon, possibly on Mars, and, weather permitting, on Venus, they will not populate these bodies, nor will they bring back, at reasonable cost, much material from them.

What we really want to know about is the nature of life and consciousness, and their meaning. Since we are where we are and what we are, the best way to continue this research is to stay on this planet and examine it more thoroughly.

Our earth may be an experiment—the only one of its kind of which we are yet, or perhaps can ever be, completely aware—and it may be our function to make it a profitable experiment. I can think of no other reason for being here except to have fun—what the philosophers call the hedonistic inclination. And having fun, on this earth, is not always easy.

The thought that we can ever completely know the universe, in this or any future generation, is foolish. Knowing the structure of matter or the relationship between energy and substance has been proven possible, but what are we to think of a "dwarf star," every cubic inch of which weighs a ton? We can never go to such a star, nor would we be happy if we did; we would be flattened like pancakes.

Man cannot, in fact, break out into space; he must stay where he has been put; there are no East Indies in the sky to which he can proceed if only he can get around Cape

Horn or the Cape of Good Hope or navigate some celestial Strait of Magellan. His knowledge of the unspeakable depths of space must ever be conjectural; his sky maps must always be like the crude charts of the first circumnavigators; he can read the immense book of the universe only in one small alcove of the infinite library of creation. He may be the wisest or perhaps the only imaginatively intelligent being in all that vast expanse, but he is not in focus, he does not even know that his five senses are all the means of perception there are, and his knowledge must forever be incomplete.

If the exploring urge takes him beyond his own tiny sphere, as it has already begun to do, he can penetrate, figuratively speaking, only to his own back fence. His heroic journeyings will be like climbing Mount Everest— an admirable exploit but more like an ant ascending a pebble than a Colossus bestriding the universe. Spatial exploration is a diversion, and a most amazing one. Our real work, when we put away childish things, is to understand and make use of the world on which we live. This is our home and habitation forever and ever; here, as God promised Noah in the Biblical story, while the earth remaineth.

It is a spacious earth, marvelously roofed with past and present stars. But I doubt that there is any Phoebe that Egbert would not rather put in a zoo than marry. We may never be sure there is any Phoebe at all.

5.

We are often told, especially in advertisements for quack remedies or cosmetics, that "science says" this or that. Science actually says nothing of the sort. Science is a method, not a doctrine, a striving for truth, not a revelation. The true scientist has taken a solemn oath, in spirit if not in word, to tell the truth, the whole truth, and nothing but the truth. He is sworn to change his mind if the evidence requires it. His great gift is an abiding inquisitiveness.

But more and more the scientist is a layman in every field but his own. Human knowledge is so vast that it has to be divided into compartments exceedingly small. A layman has no license to discuss scientific data with which he is not familiar, but he does have not only a right but a bounden duty to discuss the *effects* of applied scientific discoveries. This is why I feel free to express doubts about the moon project. I would like well enough to know whether the surface of the moon is made of sand, lava, mud, cheese, or apple pie, but I wouldn't vote to spend $20 billion trying to find out. There ought to be more multi-billion-dollar projects for the earth itself and the people thereof. There is so much still to learn about the old homestead and the curious creatures, ourselves among them, that inhabit it.

It is true that scientists in their innumerable compartments have been finding out a vast number of details about the speck of dust on which we dwell. They have probably found out more since 1900 than their predecessors during all the centuries since man became recognizably human. The surface of the globe, including the crests of the Himalayas and both poles, has been almost completely explored, and its resources have been at least charted and in many instances fully exploited. And since Freud and Jung the soul of man has been peeled like an onion. Yet, when all is considered, much remains to be found out—and it is almost desperately urgent that we do find out. So far we have done little more than does a storekeeper when he takes an inventory. We don't really know, as yet, all that we can *do* with our stock in trade. Infinite mystery lies under our feet and in the depths of the ocean, and this can be studied here and now, without waiting toe the vast parade of the light years.

What we need now is a sense of direction, which does not come from a frittering away of energies in moon shots, or planet shots or galaxy shots. Science has revolutionized our lives without planning to. Nobody invented the world we have today, nor the apparatus by which we have partially and imperfectly controlled it. There was no plan, no great coordinator. Now we need plans and coordination.

Ahead of us, on this earth, lies a task that requires the best brains and the liveliest energies of our race. I do not believe we have time enough or energy enough for the great Fourth-of-July shooting enterprises to which we have been giving so much attention.

In another thousand years or so the situation will be different. Until then we might try to be patient, doing what comes nearest to hand.

To illustrate what I mean I would like to give a chapter or two to some problems of present-day human society. One of these problems is bigness: Big Government, Big Business, Big Labor. These are small items in a vast universe, but we are small items, too—we human beings.

VIII

Army of the Potomac

IT USED TO BE SAID that every boy born in the United States had a chance to become President. This, for a few obvious reasons, was not true. But every four or eight years, a former boy does become President. The Marine Band or some other body of qualified musicians then plays *Hail to the Chief* whenever this eminent individual heaves into sight—which must be fun for the first few hundred times. Perhaps I am eccentric in my views, but I do believe that if I had a male child of suitable age I would try to calm his apprehensions by telling him he would probably never be President, and that in any case he didn't have to be. For the Presidency, in this current year, is not merely a difficult task—it is impossible. It is impossible because the Federal Government is now so big that one man cannot make all the required executive decisions.

It has been getting bigger for many years. Theodore Roosevelt "had a bully time" in the White House. Mr. Taft retired to the Supreme Court with an almost audible sigh of relief. Mr. Harding played a little poker and otherwise disported himself. Mr. Coolidge took naps after lunch.

Mr. Hoover sweated it out glumly, like the conscientious man he was. Franklin D. Roosevelt took it gaily—and died of too much of it. Mr. Eisenhower fought like a good soldier against several attacks of ill health, but he was only half-joking (so his friends said) when he spoke of the Executive Mansion as "the salt mine." Mr. Truman emerged with more jauntiness than any other President—I can't see why, for he had some terrible crises to deal with.

In recent years—notably since the death of Franklin D. Roosevelt—Presidents have chosen their Vice-Presidents (and they *do* choose them) as possible successors. Mr. Roosevelt did not take the precaution to brief the Vice-President on what he might have to deal with. Subsequent Chief Executives have been more meticulous. Mr. Nixon, Mr. Johnson, and Mr. Humphrey actually have done quite a few important errands for the man at the top—our Princes of Wales for a term or two.

But a President can't relax. The moment he is elected he becomes, whether he likes it or not, a father figure. Yesterday nobody paid much attention to him as he rode down the street or entered some public place. Overnight he becomes royalty. Seemingly it is not what he has to do that weighs him down, it is what he has to decide.

Naturally he has advisors. All our Presidents, all men in power, have had these. Jackson had his "kitchen cabinet." Lincoln had Secretary Seward, who was sure he knew more than anybody else, including the President. Wilson had Colonel House—and broke with him for reasons the Colonel either didn't know or wouldn't tell. Franklin D. Roosevelt had Harry Hopkins and others—in fact, a "Brain Trust."

Recent memoirs (writing them has become almost a major industry) show the President as the center of a vast network, which he undoubtedly is, with the narrator in each case as the principal observer, secondary actor, or Lanny Budd in the Administration, which is not always true.

A sensible President has advisors in every state, and knows just where to turn when there is a crisis in Rhode Island or Idaho. He also studies opinion polls. His press secretary can feed stories to various media and then sit innocently back, waiting for a public reaction.

2.

The President also has a vast fact-gathering, opinion-sampling, computing apparatus at his command. The whole web trembles when either the spider or the fly walks on it, and the President, with no disrespect implied, may be thought of as the spider waiting for flies. But what a cumbersome process, what an impossible procedure, it all is!

The President can ask for or stimulate all sorts of reports on all domestic or foreign problems. He will have regular communications from the Cabinet departments, in case he wants them. He can put the Secretary of State to the question, and if he has a little spare time he can be his own Secretary of State. He has speech composers and message writers at his command. He has experts to work on his budgets—and no one who even glances at a federal budget can say that it is simple, even for a President. But what does all this come to? He has to remember more than most men's heads will hold. He has to deal with conflicting opinions and decide which is correct.

If he has been a member of either House of Congress, or successively of both Houses, the President will have links of friendship and of influence in each Chamber. These he needs in his business, for if he lacks them there is often not much he can do except to sign or refuse to sign his name.

So, if he is experienced and intelligent, he works through agents, or directly with Senators and Representatives to get things done. He has people to breakfast, lunch, and dinner. He gives receptions. He gets around—he has to. He shows himself to the public—he has to. He is constantly on television. He has press conferences—if these are too few the reporters are aggrieved. He must be humorous at times, without marring his dignity. He must be kind to children and dumb animals.

He must walk a tight rope between being a deity and being a common man. If he ever forgets to be a deity the political wolves will tear him down. If he ever forgets to be a common man the boys at the drug store or the garage will disown him.

The President simply can't do all the things a President is supposed to do or be all the things a President is expected to be. The pretence is as absurd as it is when a descendant of the House of Hanover is held, by accident of birth, not by personal charm or built-in genius, to be fit for the throne of Britain. The British may be more sensible than we are, for they no longer allow their sovereign to rule.

Switzerland, which is a federal union, has a Council of seven members; of these one is chosen each year to serve a year as President. Switzerland has less than 3 percent of our population, but she doesn't even pretend that one man can run the country all alone, or for very long. I believe we would do better if we also stopped trying to believe the impossible.

Well, maybe there has to be one man who for four years or eight years symbolizes the nation. I think we might try to imagine one President and about a dozen assorted semi-Presidents. The Number One President would then be a species of Chairman of the Board, not too much involved in day-by-day operations, but making long-term plans and being looked up to (though perhaps not deified) by the public. There would be plenty of work for everybody to do, and enough responsibility to give some to each.

This plan would take the place of the present provisions for the Presidential succession. It seems to me it would be far more sensible to replace the President, in case of death or disability, by a specially trained individual than to have the usual Vice-President or the Speaker of the House next in line. For one thing, this would make it impossible for a President of one party to be followed by a Speaker of another political party, without an intervening election. I assume, of course, that the semi-Presidents would all run on the same party list as the Presidential candidate, and that the order of their succession to the hot seat in the White House would be designated in advance.

I have no little boy, but if I did have one, I might encourage him not to run for President, but to try for a place pretty far down in the substitute team. The very existence of the team would make it less probable, I should think, that any one member would be called in to take the top job. And the Marine Band might play *Hail to the Semi-Chief* whenever any of these quasi-dignitaries appeared in public.

3.

The Federal budget has now far outrun the hundred-billion-dollar limit. That is, it is more than $500 per capita. Not long ago one could live on what one now pays out in federal taxes.

Government has now become the biggest business in the United States. If you add in state and local taxes the outlay is—well, let us say—astronomical. At the moment, however, the federal outlay is enough for one day's worrying.

If you had to review every civil service federal worker in the United States you would find that they took a long time to pass a given point—they are past the 1,600,000 mark, or more than 2 percent of our national working force. Such is the new army of the Potomac. If you were to include every worker making goods for the Federal Government, the percentage would naturally be much greater. Our Federal Budget today represents about one-sixth of the goods and services that economists call the gross national product. It is reasonably safe to assume that about one-sixth of our labor force is working directly or indirectly for Washington, D.C.

I am not complaining about this. I am merely reminding the ferocious reader that the Federal Government has become a very big undertaking indeed. And most of this has happened during the lifetime of many living men. Washington is now spending approximately one hundred and fifty times as much (measured, to be sure, in depreciated dollars) as it did at the beginning of the First World War.

It is spending more, of course, because it is doing more. Much of this, as I was noting, goes to what is called de-

fense. Some goes to pay for past wars that we did not succeed in preventing. The Government has been passing out
cash or its equivalent for what is called foreign aid. This
has not always been efficiently administered, but the idea
was and is a good one, and I have been among the men in
the street who cheerfully supported it. However, it did
send our taxes up a little. Washington itself has nothing to
give or lend; the taxpayers do the paying.

The Government has done and is doing quite a few other
things: it has paid farmers to let land lie fallow and has
taken surplus food products (in this hungry world) off the
market; it has subsidized shipping; it has constructed dams
and irrigation systems; it has aided low-rent housing; it has
pensioned veterans from all our recent wars; it has tried to
keep our food and drugs pure; it has regulated us in various
ways whenever we crossed state lines for good or dubious
purposes; it maintains parks, national monuments, and rec-
reational areas; it has kept a fatherly eye on the forests and
wild game; it had dredged rivers and harbors (nothing new
in that); it has taken jurisdiction over the use of the air
waves for radio and television and of the air itself for passenger flight and freight carriage; it decides who gets into
the United States and sometimes who gets out; it is now en-
forcing civil rights where it can and where the states do
not; it takes a hand in any labor dispute affecting interstate
commerce; it aids education; it has built or helped build a
far-reaching web of highways; it has organized an amazing
system of social security, including Medicare; it has en-
couraged science in various ways. It does all these things
and many more, in addition to the enormous mass of activities grouped under the general head of defense.

The scope of the Federal Government today goes infinitely beyond anything George Washington or Thomas Jefferson could have contemplated. It probably goes far beyond anything the original Thirteen Colonies would have ratified in 1789. But the work the Federal Government does had to be done by somebody. The states, much less the local governments, weren't up to it, any more than an old-fashioned iron foundry is up to making structural steel.

It should do us good to bear in mind that at any level, the Government is people. At any level it may be good or bad. One town clerk in a New England village, one county judge in California, one sheriff in Alabama may be just as mean and stuffy as a clerk in the circumlocution office in Washington. States' rights is a noble phrase, but sometimes it may be just a cover-up for the right of a minority to run the state or the town. In times and in places the more rights the states have, the fewer rights many individuals have.

We have to delegate power to some agent. The United States is too big to be run like an old-fashioned town meeting.

4.

Our nation has been thrust, almost against its will, into a position of world leadership. We are, after our fashion, an Empire—a reluctant one and by no means one cast in the old pattern. A few nations have needed the help of our soldiers; many more have welcomed our Peace Corps and similar activities. These overseas adventures have to be managed and directed from Washington—another phase of Big Government. So here we are—in many ways an old-fashioned people in a new-fashioned world in which the small farm, the small factory, and the small store are lost. We are increasingly members and associates in a great community. John Jones may live on a subsistence farm on the Cumberland Plateau in Tennessee, in the Green Mountains of Vermont, or on an Imperial Valley date ranch in California; he may work in a factory in Detroit; he may run a second-hand store on the lower Bowery in New York City; but he cannot effectively act outside our national boundaries, or in large matters inside the boundaries, except through the Federal Government.

He cannot run a railroad or a bus line; he cannot provide education for his children, he cannot maintain the public health, on his own accord, as an individual. We are all caught in the net of interdependence, and the net will grow bigger and more tightly woven whether we like it or not.

To do large things and achieve major aims we have to work through a big-scale Government. I am sorry this is so. I think I am as sorry as Mr. Goldwater was when he was in the 1964 Presidential campaign. But being sorry doesn't get anybody anywhere at any time. There cannot be a re-play of the past, as there can with a phonograph record.

At the time of the American Revolution the farmer and his family were about 90 percent of the population. Today the percentage is down to seven. So the farm traditions are dying. There are new traditions and new worries, and a new kind of America to deal with them.

5.

This cannot be done by the citizens of any one state; that task will require the whole Union of States—that is, the

Federal Government. I chuckle in my beard when I hear people speak of that agency of the whole people as though it were something imposed upon them by conquest. The office-holders are like ourselves in every respect except that they follow a different trade or profession. At intervals not too widely spaced, we have the chance to throw the rascals out and put in rascals of our later choosing. Good or bad, the army of the Potomac is essential to the smooth workings of the national economy. Some necessary things can be done only in Washington.

What do State boundaries mean when it takes only a few hours to cross the continent? Today's Senator or Representative is just the old County Supervisor writ large. Washington and such of its inhabitants as work for the Federal Government, the long, the short, and the wide, are just ourselves, no more and no less. No individual is changed in any inward and essential respect when he goes to work for Uncle Sam; and this is true whether he is among the brass hats or is one of the humblest privates. He is not an enemy or an alien to the rest of us; he—or she—simply has a somewhat different job.

And the rank-and-file federal job may not be greatly different from one in private industry or business. All large offices these days use the same machinery that the Federal Government does. The federal employee may not have to make a profit for anybody, but he is under pressure (far more than he used to be) not to waste what is jocosely called "the taxpayer's money."

Washington may grow arrogant—it sometimes does. So do some other concerns and public utilities, though they are privately owned. Big business is big business, whether privately or publicly owned and controlled; and the burden of my sad song is that since it is more efficient than little business we are stuck with it.

I do not see any way out of this dilemma, not at the moment.

Big business is the price of economy in time, work, and money. George Washington and John Adams could operate as Presidents with a staff that today wouldn't be enough to run a dry cleaning establishment. They could do this with quill pens, imperfect paper and ink, and totally inadequate communication. We now have a Big Government, not because we like it—I don't believe we do—but because there is so much work on hand and no other way to do it. Why does the Government do this work? Because we the people, directly or through our representatives, have told it to.

Bigness, concentration, and specialization are essentials for successful government today in a country as large and well-peopled as the United States. The bureaucracy that works in today's Washington and that branches out from that city into every community, was not invented by men who happened at the time to be feeling especially mean and vindictive. Nor did it come about in a burst of careless frivolity. It grew like a cabbage.

It grew because otherwise something bigger and less responsible would have made the rules and run the country: private Big Business, sometimes fighting Big Labor and sometimes in alliance with it. Let us turn a page or two and examine these other kinds of big operations.

IX

·········

Big Business,
Big Labor

I AM TEMPTED to do some colorful prose to the effect
that bigness comes naturally to a people inhabiting the vast
terrain of North America, dwelling in the shadows of lofty
mountains, resting their eyes on seemingly limitless prairies
and plains, watching the majestic procession of mighty
rivers. Our part of this continent is indeed a mighty assembly line, stretching from sea to sea.

But the purple prose would explain nothing. Russia had
these things and Britain didn't; yet it was from little
Britain, not vast Russia, that we took over the industrial
revolution—and revolutionized it, in a few swift decades,
into the age of automation.

This process could no more be stopped than could the
sweep of winds across the Dakotas. It was not the work of
a few great men. Man himself, in his irresistible instinct to
throw his weight around, brought it to pass. It was a folk
achievement in a new, sparsely inhabited country. It began
in simplicity; it has developed into an extraordinary com-

plexity. In the climate and culture of the Indian Peninsula we might have sprawled out, as the East Indians did, into a succession of countless villages, sprinkled on the land, a few hundred yards distant one from the other. This didn't happen. We built mighty cities and innumerable small cities and towns. We turned to labor-saving machinery. We multiplied and specialized.

As our population approached 200 million, we developed bigger and more intricate corporations, and to offset these, bigger and bigger labor unions. Corporations and labor unions alike sometimes behaved like perfect gentlemen and sometimes like bloodthirsty rowdies. Just like individuals, one might say. But they did become a system.

The corporation is a risk-sharing device, not especially new. The Romans had something at least remotely resembling it. In fairly modern times the corporation—sometimes called a "company of merchant adventurers"—was useful in colonizing and other imperialistic undertakings.

But the corporation as we know it did not really get going until the nineteenth century, when it had to deal with efficient, large-scale machinery and with vast natural resources. Railroads had to assume the corporate form. At first they could be rather small corporations, for they often extended merely from one body of water—a river, canal, or lake—to another. Their titles were full of local allusions —Delaware and Hudson, New York, New Haven, and Hartford, and all the "Centrals" of Vermont, Michigan, and so on.

The great Western lines—Union Pacific, Southern Pacific, Central Pacific, Great Northern—had names reflecting a greater geographical sweep. But even here we have the Santa Fe and the Denver and Rio Grande.

Today the great trunk lines, with the blessing of the Interstate Commerce Commission, are evolving into even mightier networks. The railroad may be tooting its way into oblivion, but the common-sense theory that bigness pays has finally been driven home. It took less than a century and a half to prove this—possibly, in the case of the railroads, a little too late. But consolidation—fewer and bigger railroad webs—may be the shot in the arm that will diminish the symptoms of their ailments—these symptoms being largely private automobiles, trucks, and airplanes.

Bigness is of course a modern trait of many other industries that are not having as much trouble as the railroads are—maybe no trouble at all. Our ideas regarding these giants have to be modified, I imagine. At the turn of the century the United States Steel Corporation was popularly believed to be worth a billion dollars. This seemed an alarming concentration of wealth. Now, as I run down the list of outstanding American business enterprises, I find two well past the billion mark in retained net income, and one, General Motors, made a profit of two billion dollars or more in 1965. (Make allowances for a depreciated currency, if you like; this is still a lot of money.)

The corporation or "trust" acquired a bad reputation during the last quarter of the nineteenth century and held it well into the present century. What was in the mind, however, of the man in the street, as he fondly nursed his grievances, was not so much the "trust" itself as the frequent abuses of its power. Some of the majestic creatures who presided over them regarded themselves as only a little lower than the angels. There was much popular disagreement with this point of view.

Hence, beginning with the Sherman Anti-Trust Act of 1890 and continuing through the reigns of Roosevelts I and II and later, we have had restrictive legislation requiring corporations to be honest, kind, true, and competitive when doing business across state lines. And not too big, either.

But the Government cannot resist natural tendencies, unless it is an absolute dictatorship. If a trust saves the consumer money it cannot be, as the saying goes, busted. If it cheats too flagrantly, another trust will bust it. In recent years every large business enterprise has hired expensive publicity men and advertising agencies to give it a good "image" with the public. Competition is rarely abolished; it merely operates on a larger scale; it has been stated that two hundred corporations dominate more than half the wealth of the United States.

There may be competition among products. For example, you may heat your house with coal, oil, gas, or in some areas, electricity. There may be competition in "service," as there appears to be among the great air lines. One should remember, too, that a corporation's securities may be widely distributed, so that if enough stockholders want to reform the management they can at least make a loud yowl about it.

2.

The rise of any strong force in a country with democratic institutions and traditions is likely to bring up an opposing force. In our time in the United States one such force is industrially organized labor. This is a fairly recent and impressively powerful upsurge.

The ancient theory that laborers who combined to raise their own wages were guilty of conspiracy has been discredited for about a century and a half. Yet between our Civil War and the administrations of Franklin D. Roosevelt there were numerous instances of the brusque and often violent suppression of labor movements in certain fields. The motor industry, for instance, fought unionism to the last, sometimes with lawless violence; then it gave in—and lived happy ever after.

I once saw Samuel Gompers, the venerable apotheosis of the American Federation of Labor, walking down Fifth Avenue in New York City. He was a chunky, readily recognizable, and successful-looking man. Gompers organized certain skilled trades most ably; he did not care to come to grips with the greater problem of the unskilled and semi-skilled. Hence he was considered respectable, even by employers. But in 1942 he walked along and out of history; and I am afraid we have to think of him as an exponent of special privilege for certain selected groups of skilled workers.

The new labor leaders were such men as John L. Lewis and the Reuther brothers. These men were able to do quite comfortably what the Black Death had done in a horrible way in Western Europe during the fourteenth century: they could produce an artificial scarcity of labor. Good or bad, this was one of the major discoveries—one might say inventions—of our time. Please note that it occurred under what the left-wingers call the capitalistic system and what others like to describe as free enterprise.

It was not quite either one, of course; our society is not

and has not been run by formulas. Workingmen, like other people, come in all shapes, sizes, and dispositions. They have just as much original sin as have captains of industry. To consider them in any other way is to revert to the strange superstitions of a century or more ago, or to the quaint theology of the Russian Revolution.

There is no longer any proletariat—not in this country, not in Western Europe. I am not sure there has ever been any in those places since feudalism died; there has been much misery and injustice, but nobody eternally doomed by the social system to misery and injustice. Today there is so much diversity among those who work with their hands, at wages ranging from about a dollar and a half an hour to five or six dollars an hour or more, that some of these "prisoners of starvation" would rather be dictated to by an employer than coerced by an arbitrary union leader. It is not free enterprise that makes some men join unions; they do it because they have to.

When I say this am I belittling the doctrine and practice of unionism? Of course not. I believe in labor unions, as I do in corporations, in their proper use, not their occasional or even habitual folly. Or I might say, I do not believe in non-unionism, especially in large, tightly organized industries. You cannot, however, create an effective labor union unless you can when necessary coerce men into joining, paying dues, and obeying strike orders issued after a majority vote.

I don't believe members of employers' associations, Chambers of Commerce, or informal, unwritten cartels are in a much different situation. Even if you merely commute in a private club car or wish to join an exclusive country club, you may not dare to differ too much from the rest of the pack; it just isn't gentlemanly. If people in an economic group don't stand together they are powerless against those who are united; if most of the automobile manufacturers or most of the wholesale lumbermen sign with the union it is prudent for the others to do so.

What is certain is that organized labor has become a third force in this country, counting management and Government as the other two. Since no individual who has not been convicted of crime can be forced to work against his will, the power to make him stop working is a tremendous one.

A strike is, of course, something like a war. Each dispenses with reason and relies on the relative amount of damage each party can inflict upon the other (or, in some cases, on the general public). The party who is hurt most, eventually gives in, and in times past this has often been the strikers and their women and children. The balance is more even now.

It is clear that some strikes hurt the innocent bystander more than others do. The public can endure a strike of diamond cutters, perfumers, necktie makers, or even actors without much hardship. A brief interruption in the flow of motor vehicles from the factories or of structural steel production may not be immediately perceptible, though the long-term effects can be bad. We can do without newspapers, though a general newspaper strike in a large city may slow down the whole community. We cannot long do without public transportation, though the inhabitants of such cities as New York have shown much ingenuity in getting around when the buses, the taxis, or even the subways were suddenly cut off. We could not endure a strike that stopped our electric power or our water supply or paralyzed our police and fire potection.

Some work has to be done without cessation, day in and day out, hour in and hour out; and if a strike is threatened in such cases Government must override the interests of management or labor or both. Such strikes or lockouts are like gang wars in the streets. It is a sound rule, though not always lived up to, that those who undertake essential functions must agree to settle their disputes in some other way than by economic warfare. An individual water-works employee, policeman, or fireman may be free to resign, but such men can't have the freedom to resign or take a vacation collectively, and in collusion to browbeat the public. Nor can physicians or nurses; we should make amends to them, but we surely must insist they do not let us down.

In most occupations, however, the unions will retain vast power. Employers today, recognizing this truth, do not resort to the strike-breaking tactics that were common only a few years ago. It is taken for granted that in most industries the unions will continue to exist; since this is so, the employers do not create a permanent breach. In the end each side, each set of negotiators, has in mind a concluding scene around a conference table, in which a document will be signed and hands shaken.

The unions, in other words, are just as much in business as the employers are. Unless we revert to the make-believe unionism under which Mussolini, Stalin, and Hitler thinly veiled their tyrannies, labor organizations will remain an accepted part of the industrial machinery. And where does this put us?

3.

It leaves us, I should say, with a new breed of captains of industry, as we used to call the big business men. These new men of power are not directly manipulating raw materials, finished goods, or services; they are controlling men. They insist that labor is not a commodity, but they often deal with it as though it were.

Labor leaders, like other dominant creatures, are often tempted to abuse their power. What about Mr. X, somebody asks; he controls a strong key union; he is also in jail for misappropriating its funds; the majority of his followers do not seem to mind this, and they go right on re-electing him.

What about Mr. Y? Mr. Y is strongly suspected of making shady deals with the employers, through which he personally profits but which do not do his union any real good. However, he has persuaded his, so to speak, fellow workers that he will not let them be kicked around by the exploiting classes. At that, maybe they are better off than they used to be, fewer patches on their pants, more rubber heels on their shoes.

What about Mr. Z? He is politically active, and even undertakes to deliver the vote of his faithful flock. It is softly whispered that he has been involved in some off-the-record deals, too.

Do the errors of Messrs X, Y, and Z prove that unionism is wrong and that we would be better off without it? No, they show that human beings are human. Their errors are of the same variety that are made by Messrs A, B, and C, who are members of Congress; by Messrs C, D, and E, who are Mayors, Governors, and even members of the Bench; or, I venture to say, under my breath, by Generals and Admirals F, G, H, and so on down the alphabet, who compete with one another for a whack at the taxpayer's dollar and once in a while a bit of aggrandizement for themselves. No matter how good our institutions are, we must always expect some frailties from those who operate them. Institutions, like automobiles, are no better in a pinch than those who drive them.

The more we can divest ourselves of the emotional sedative or stimulant embodied in such capsule words as labor and capital the more sensible we may become. The laboring man today is likely to be a capitalist in a modest way, even though he is merely participating in a pension plan for his old age or buying a little insurance. I read in my newspaper this morning that pay and fringe benefits in a new union contract for plumbers in the San Francisco Bay area are approaching $372 a week. I am glad the plumbers are doing well, but I don't regard them as proletarians and I am not sorry for them.

Labor doesn't even dress the part any more. In large and stable enterprises it does not eat from a full dinner pail kept warm on a steam boiler but goes to the cafeteria. When labor has a chance, which is pretty often, it has a shower and changes its clothes in the locker room before it goes home. Sometimes it takes a tailor or a head waiter to tell whether a given individual is a prisoner of starvation or a malefactor of great wealth.

We are not an equalitarian society—not even in opportunities. In spite of taxes, the principle of inheritance still discriminates among us, so that some young people start in life with an advantage over other young people. Or is it an advantage not to have to flex one's muscles?

We do not have a racial equality of opportunity, either, though federal laws and some state laws say we do; yet the very "best" society in the land does not rest on inherited wealth but on achievement. We admittedly worship success; I think this is less vulgar than worshiping ancestry. In what is perhaps a pioneer tradition we think highly of creativity. On the other hand, we especially like this when it is demonstrably well-paid; an artist in a garret does not fascinate us half so much as an artist or actor or author of a best seller or a television personality dining at a costly restaurant. We like bold, flashing figures rising out of the dust and thumbing their noses at fate.

We don't have incurable accents, not in the United States, that label us as soon as we open our mouths. We can easily learn, even if we have to read a book, how to use our knives and forks in an acceptable manner. Don't ask me why we read so avidly in the society columns about the dreary doings of the ostentatiously affluent. Or why we read the sports columns, though we may not ourselves indulge in strenuous exercise.

The "capitalists" and the "masses," the employers and the "workers" seethe and boil and change roles in a manner that even that great Virginian Jacobin, Thomas Jefferson, could never have foreseen—let alone Karl Marx.

We are not a static society, and I trust we never will be. But I suspect there are in our community as in others three sorts of individuals (not classes): those who enjoy managing things; those often creative types who don't care to manage but who refuse to be managed; and those who don't mind being managed, provided they are sure of their meals and lodging. Our society does pretty well by all of these.

I have often played with the thought of a wicked—or perhaps merely experimental—godmother exchanging babies in the nursery. I doubt whether it would make much difference whether she gave her favorite power over others as employer, labor leader, or politician—it's the power that counts. The babies would coo and gurgle at the prospect of power, no matter what kind; they would shake it like a rattle at the happily unsuspecting world.

One might dissect the power impulse more than I have done or intend to do. There is a hierarchy in business, in politics, and in labor whose members recognize one another when they meet. I suppose, also, each concedes that the others are necessary to our system. Our great organizations in these three primary fields will not function without an almost military delegation of authority. If any one of these gets out of balance we will have trouble.

The future is likely to produce a tighter set of organizations, not looser ones. To hold its own against them, liberty will conceivably have to be defended and if necessary won back every year, beginning just after midnight on the first of January and ending just before midnight on the thirty-first of December.

It will not be easy.

X

·—·—·—·

By the Sweat of our Brows

NO, IT WILL NOT be easy to keep liberty alive in the tightly integrated society of the future. I think, however, we can get rid of two fallacies that have been plaguing us. One of these superstitions is that jobs—that is, masses of men and women working for wages—are essential to our civilization, even to our physical survival. The other is that automatic processes crush individualism.

A child in grammar school should know better—and some day will know better. In this chapter I would like to point out some economic aspects of the job fetish. In the next I expect to pick up the psychological results of having machinery do for us a kind of work we don't like to do for ourselves—automation, in fact. Since I do not pretend to be either an economist or a psychologist, these reflections should be good clean fun, not contaminated by pedantry.

Just us grocery-store philosophers talking around the stove, in fact. Or maybe around the radiator.

I will begin, as I believe the Devil does, by quoting from Scripture. We are told in the third chapter of the Book of Genesis that the Lord God said to Adam, who had been robbing apple orchards, "In the sweat of thy face shalt thou eat bread." As Adam's children multiplied, some got bread and even cake, without sweating, and others had to perspire to some extent. This was called the division of labor.

But Adam and Eve themselves went to work—they had to. So the generations flowed by. Let us jump some thousands of years. In England, in the late fourteenth century, a seditious, un-British, left-wing rhyme was attributed to John Ball: "When Adam delved and Eve span, who then was the gentleman?" The so-called curse of Adam seemed honorable in John Ball's eyes; he assailed the British nobility because they were so richly rewarded for not doing what the Lord God had ordered. The lords of the realm (who are not to be confused with the Lord God) suppressed this heresy with great slaughter. They themselves then continued not to work, although if provided with weapons and heavy armor they would cheerfully defend their country by going off to a foolish war. They were brave men, but it was the infantry, as usual, who were wounded or killed. Later the nobility took up fox hunting.

But the doctrine that work is a good thing for most of us did not die. It seems to have been re-invigorated at about the time of the Protestant Reformation, in the early sixteenth century. Medieval labor had never been well-fed, well-paid, well-housed, or (except as it received the "humbles" or insides of certain meat animals) well-fed. Hence, it had no inducement to work harder than it was compelled to. Moreover, its pious masters had allowed it many days off each year, including Sundays and saints' days. (Holiday, of course, is merely a contraction of "saint's day"—that is, "holy day.") The Reformation created or reflected a new attitude toward work.

The first signs of what came to be called the Industrial Revolution appeared in the new-fledged Protestant countries—Scandinavia, the Netherlands, parts of Germany, and above all, Britain. The great god work was worshiped in addition to other and less demanding deities. In ordering us not to work on the seventh day the commandment seemed to be laying out a six-day week—and a working day that ran from dawn to dusk.

It was seen at once that work was not only a godly act but that it paid dividends, especially if it were done for as little pay as possible by some one other than oneself. Work on a farm, in a cottage, or (after many generations) in a factory, raised the general standard of living.

The earlier enthusiasm for the virtues of work was revived in latter-day pioneer communities. The English, for example, found work an excellent thing when they went pioneering in New England and Virginia. Purely decorative colonists were of little use, even though they came from the best families.

Yet, curiously enough, it was during the early pioneering period—the original Elizabethan Age—that the Welfare State first showed its controversial head. By the year 1601 Elizabeth's government had established the principle that the well-to-do should be taxed to support the incapacitated poor (later even the "undeserving poor," as Shaw called them in *Pygmalion*) and that some provision should be made to house the unemployed members of the working population and give them something to do—hence the term "work-house." I suppose some of the modern Marxian attitudes toward "workers," "toilers," and so on are connected with this Puritanic conception. The "workingman" was regarded by modern revolutionists as a repository of all virtues and all wisdom. He was called upon to unite and told that he had a world to gain and nothing to lose but his chains.

2.

Benjamin Franklin gathered up a batch of aphorisms and printed them in *Poor Richard's Almanac*. One of them was, "Early to bed and early to rise makes a man healthy, wealthy, and wise." Of course it does no such thing. It depends on the man's job, or whether he works best by day or by night.

I think Franklin copied down this and other platitudes with his tongue in his cheek. But he was followed by Samuel Smiles, by some didactic New England poets, by the Alger boys, and a few others. All of these argued, by precept or example, that the way to get ahead in the world is to work hard and save money.

But nobody ever gets rich in this fashion. Try it some time and see. Mr. Franklin let on to think, in his Poor Richard phase, that it doesn't matter what we do as long as we do something. This is childish. It is far better to hire somebody else to do it, and then pay him a little less than he is worth. Or it may be possible to invent a gadget that will do it. One of the early gadgets in the Watts steam engine is said to have originated with a boy who got tired of pulling a lever; he tied a string to a moving part of the engine and went fishing.

Franklin was widely applauded. The applause was earned by his scientific experiments, his diplomatic skill, his literary art, and his magnificent autobiography, not by his axiomatic wisecracks. I wouldn't willingly expose my theoretical son to his Poor Richard nonsense.

A richer field for exploitation than any amount of penny-saving and early rising was provided in this country by the immigrants, flooding in by thousands, then by hundreds of thousands, and finally, by the time of the First World War, by millions. The rich returns here, of course, were gained by chicanery rather than by sweat. The early arrivals and the natives found the immigrants exceedingly profitable. The more so, perhaps, because the immigrants, having read *Poor Richard* in their native tongues, thought the way to get ahead in their new homes was to work long hours for poor pay. The great lesson of our nineteenth century industry is that physical work doesn't really lead to wealth.

What yields the highest reward is and has been selling, organizing, inventing, planning—the use of one's wits rather than one's muscles. Let us not be dismayed; it is by the use of our wits that we have outdistanced the other primates.

Perhaps the most glittering example in our history of thrift and hard work combined with extraordinary business acumen is that of the elder John D. Rockefeller (1839–1932). But it wasn't his thrift that made it unnecessary for Mr. Rockefeller to be thrifty in his old age; it was a combination of organizing genius and good luck.

But what is Mr. Rockefeller best remembered for, by those to whom he is more than a fabulous name? I have no doubt at all that what lingers is his habit, acquired in his later years, of giving away dimes.

So we have the dramatic contrast: on the one hand, we

sing the virtues of thrift, sweat, and toil. On the
other hand, we have idealized the great gamblers, the men
who bet their bottom dollars, the pioneers in new territory
and new businesses. The hardships of the great overland
pioneer trails were offset in men's minds by the pot of gold
that might be found at the end of the rainbow. We haven't
so much wanted jobs as we have desired a profitable opportunity to manipulate Nature and our fellowmen.

3.

Yet the economic hell that many men have feared was
unemployment, as though men might die, not of overwork
but of underwork. I can see why a proud individual might
worry about this. I can't, for the life of me, see how a
whole society can worry about it. Whole societies, like the
American Indians, the South Sea Islanders and even our
own ancestors during the Middle Ages have subsisted without anybody worrying about a job. (The women often did
the work, of course.) People worked when they were able,
because if of sufficiently low degree, they were made to.
When they were too old or sick to work they didn't.

Depressions and unemployment are comparatively modern inventions, but they are already out of date. So is the
Spartan fortitude with which many of the prosperous used
to relax in comfort while the unemployed poor went
hungry or suffered grievous humiliations. This patient en-
durance of other people's sorrows today seems fatuous as
well as cruel. I haven't lately heard any intelligent person
say that "anybody who wants a job can get one." It is too
clear that not everybody can. The Social Security system
doesn't prevent unemployment, because it can't, but it does

cushion the shock of the resulting wage losses. And it isn't joblessness that hurts most—it's not having any money. Perhaps also not being needed or wanted.

Employment is hard to measure statistically. The unemployed may include those with seasonal jobs, such as construction workers in some states; those who are between jobs; those who have finished school but haven't been fitted into the labor force, and actually, though not statistically, many who are ill, or taking a voluntary vacation or (in increasing numbers) have retired.

The figures, such as they are, vary enormously and naturally tend to increase with population. At the bottom of the great depression that began in 1929 the jobless may have been as high as thirteen million—the number that a few years later we were able to take out of the population and put into the armed services. I shan't attempt to explain this numerical coincidence.

A more rational society would have regarded the peacetime surplus of goods and laborers as an asset, but it was in fact treated as a catastrophic deficit. Our society was in the plight of Midas: we were starving because our food had turned to gold. Men went hungry because there was too much to eat, ragged because of an over-production of clothing, homeless because there were too many houses.

We have learned a great deal since the 1929 depression. Yet many of us still cling to the fantasy that it is the job problem, not the goods-and-services problem, that has to be solved. Emotionally, perhaps, it does have to be solved; economically it is of no consequence whatsoever. There is much to be said in favor of jobs. But to suggest that it is a calamity for a nation to be able to produce enough goods and render needed services without using all its available labor is, as we used to say in my home town, horse feathers.

The late Charles M. Schwab, first president of the U.S. Steel Company, said his concern couldn't profitably turn out steel on anything less than a twelve-hour, seven-day labor week. He was sorry about this, for he was a kind-hearted man. However, you *could* manufacture steel in a more civilized way, when you had to—which was when the steel workers successfully organized and demanded a three-shift, eight-hour day. And now we have steel mills that are so nearly automatic that hardly anybody has to work up a sweat. More machines, fewer men: is that a catastrophe?

But labor leaders, in steel and other industries, continued to argue that the shorter the working day and working week the less unemployment. They warmly and generously advocated a policy of "sharing the jobs." They didn't realize that the true problem was not to produce less ham and eggs per laborer but to set up a distribution system that would provide ham and eggs for all who needed them.

Employers and "workers" alike have long been thinking of jobs as the great objective toward which all creation moved, the ultimate shining goal of human society. Few seem to have paused to reflect that there would now be more jobs if all labor-saving devices had been forbidden by law—as some, indeed, have been forbidden in labor contracts. More jobs, and fewer things to eat, wear, and enjoy.

Then came what has been called automation, the feed-back principle, or to be really high-toned about it all, cybernetics. These are lovely new names for an old principle: never do by hand what you can do with a machine; never walk when you can ride. The curse of Adam has been repealed.

One would have expected some dancing in the streets to celebrate this marvel. But there wasn't.

4.

The Greeks of the Golden Age in Athens, more than two thousand years ago, had few machines other than the human ones known as slaves. This was not as a rule a golden age for the slaves, but the masters could—and sometimes did—think the noblest thoughts of all secular history.

In our own days we have all heard the argument that an aristocracy or leisure class is good medicine for a society, since it gives at least a few people the opportunity to preserve and enhance the cultural heritage. Some of the photographs shown in the society columns may raise doubts about this. But never mind—let us examine some scraps of evidence. You just can't tell. Shakespeare probably had a small amount of cash when he went up to London to try his luck in the theatre. I doubt that he had to call on Mr. Bacon as his collaborator. Samuel Johnson started poor and had to do hack jobs to make a living. Charles Darwin didn't have to earn his daily bread. Byron was a lord, but Keats was for a time an apothecary's apprentice. Dickens as a boy worked in a blacking factory. Patient merit can never succeed in the world unless it has the mental and physical stamina and some luck. Genius is seemingly distributed rather evenly through the population, rich and poor, of ancient lineage or modern enterprise; you have it or you don't, and it can't be bequeathed. Or bought.

The best we can do about this is to organize our society so that everybody will have enough spare time and enough spare energy to develop whatever creative talents he possesses. What we now call unemployment is one way to make this possible: instead of letting men rot in idleness, let us make use of them. This is now economically possible.

We don't even have to rob the rich in order to give leisure to the impoverished: what with federal taxes and the necessity for what Veblen called "conspicuous expenditure" the poor dears have enough to put up with. And since they are, like the plumbers and the other oppressed trades, of the stuff of common humanity, we need their talents.

Our laboring classes, the exploited of the earth, are more and more being made of metal and activated by electricity. The machine has captured us and set us free. Why be afraid? Why ask, as the I. W. W. did so long ago, "How the hell can we work when there's no work to do?" It is curious, indeed, that a race clever enough to invent machines should be stupid enough to be frightened of them, and disorganized enough to be unable to make full use of the blessings they bring. I suppose this is where Freudianism and other upsetting theories come in. We are just as childish as our remote ancestors, only in a different way. They ran from the sabre-toothed tiger, we run from the computer; they found it hard to get enough to eat; we find it hard to get enough work to do.

What we must do, cruel and remorseless as it may seem,

is to enslave the machine; make it work twenty-four hours a day; send it to be melted down when we are through with it.

And we must keep a sense of proportion. Men will continue to ride herd on the machines. We shall not live the lives of the legendary South Sea Islander, who dug yams with his toe and picked up coconuts if they fell near enough his hammock. Somebody will have to watch dials, turn switches, answer incoming mail, or in Gilbert's immortal phrase, polish up the handle of the big front door. We shall need night watchmen, policemen, postmen, salesmen, physicians, and spiritual advisers. An automatic engine cannot sell me a split-level house, arrange a will or a mortgage, fix up the plumbing and the insurance—and quite a few other things.

We don't have to dig ditches any more with a shovel, carry heavy weights, shovel coal into a furnace, hammer nails or do many kinds of cooking, but if we drink we usually need good bartenders—or good friends. Housewives don't have to soak the tapioca over night when they want to make a pudding, or start the oatmeal simmering while they do the dishes—by hand. People no longer sweep carpets with a broom, take them outdoors and beat them on a line, or even use carpet sweepers; the vacuum cleaner—or perhaps a built-in suction draft—will take care of the situation. Is the housewife thereby cast into the ranks of the unemployed? No, she watches television, reads a good book, plays on the piano, or goes to the woman's club. The things we are going to have, from household appliances to automobiles, are largely projections of things we already have.

And what horrible fate threatens us? More leisure, I should say. More time for fun and self-improvement. The stern gospel of work won't draw much of a crowd when the man lectures on it in Hyde Park or Union Square.

At the moment millions of the people of India, Pakistan, Central Africa, and many of the Latin American lands and the islands of the Pacific do not have enough to eat, adequate housing, suitable clothing, good doctoring, or good nursing; they are not worrying about a superfluity of labor-saving devices but about the lack of them. Or should I say, the poverty that is caused by the lack of them? They yearn for what we Occidentals already have and take for granted. If and when they get it most of the tragic tensions of today's international politics will diminish.

I realize that I have not solved the personal problems of those who can find no work to do. What I am certain of is that mankind will not starve to death because it has too much to eat.

A part of the old risk of joblessness—or rather of wage-lessness—has been solved by unemployment compensation and it is hard to see why insurance in some form or other shouldn't take it all. It could be something better than what the British long ago adopted and called the "dole."

There are some psychological aspects of joblessness that I would like to glance at in the next chapter. These are part of the vast problem of the individual in a machine economy.

XI

········

The Job of Being Free

IF I WERE to be asked, what is an individual, I wouldn't be able to say. I suppose there can be no such thing as a sane person completely detached from his fellows and their institutions. How normal was Robinson Crusoe when they took him off the island?

We do hear today, however, that something called individualism, which is usually hooked up with something else called free enterprise, is in peril. This is one of the myths of our time, and is commonly uttered with an air of great wisdom after a good dinner. It is akin, I think, to the belief in witchcraft held by many in earlier periods. It is also related to the uncomfortable young who call themselves Beatniks and let their hair grow. In trying not to be like anybody else they become the more intensely like one another; and in the end are less individualistic than at the beginning.

In fact, neither the sedate businessmen who lament free enterprise, nor the young who jeer at their professors, have anything new and awful to complain about. As far as I can tell, man has never been perfectly free at any time in his history to be utterly an individual. In a state of nature a member of our species must have been about as free as a clam enjoying a brisk social life with other clams. (As we all know, a clam doesn't dare do anything really original.)

Primitive tribes, all the way from the mountains of New Guinea to the uplands of Kenya, or some racially fanatical backwaters of our own southland, have always had hard and fast traditional ways, from which it was—and is— unwise and even suicidal for an individual to depart. If you were a woman and wanted to stay alive you wouldn't eat bananas in old Hawaii. If you belonged to the sweeper caste in India you didn't dare let your shadow fall on a high-caste Brahmin. Social customs, religious practices, tabus of various sorts, prescribed rules for any person who proposed to catch a fish, plant a yam, or go on a journey—all these hampered us for generations. One may truthfully say that in all early or primitive societies a man or a woman was on probation during an entire lifetime.

Man may not have had as many enslaving instincts as the other creatures; to take their places he invented communal instincts. To this hour we are haunted by memories of our aboriginal ways; this is why we read of such lawless adventures as those of Huck Finn and Tom Sawyer with delight. On a more sinister level this is why criminals revolt against society; they are primitive, often solitary savages some thousands of years too late.

The conditions under which human beings have always lived have compelled them to organize—maybe first in families, later in clans, then in nations, finally in vast conglomerations. And organization always means some loss, voluntary or otherwise, of individual freedom.

Can we at last build a community in which the machines

alone will have to be rigidly disciplined, and the individual will have room in which to breathe freely and think his own thoughts?

I think we now have more chance to do this than we ever had before.

2.

Cultural history is full of the biographies of persons who tried to break out of the crowd. Of many of these experiments, no doubt, we have not and will never have an account. Hermits, philosophers, star-watchers, saints, eccentrics, trappers, prospectors, explorers, all were weary of the enforced routine of community life. The challenge of new lands has often been merely a rejection of the old ways and habits. Who settled America? Not merely the tired the poor, the huddled masses yearning to be free, the homeless, the tempest-tossed (to paraphrase Emily Lazarus' compassionate and famous lines), not only these, but those who believed they would find a new freedom and a spiritual spaciousness in a new land. How stuffy Concord was! So many must have thought of that town or a thousand others, how stuffy! People wanted to get where they could breathe freely.

The fur trade in the Rockies was dying when Thoreau was at Walden Pond, but scores, hundreds and eventually thousands, of pioneers were slogging westward into California; some of these may have looked upon that future state as a huge utopia—which it never was. But the Walden Pond variety of individualism wasn't sweeping the country.

The individualism we did fall into wasn't Thoreau's. It wasn't the genuine article. It was brassy, booming, and exceedingly self-satisfied. The doctrine, as customarily expressed, was not "do without," but "grab or knuckle under." It upheld the right of the "superior" individual to dictate to the "inferior" and less free individuals and tribes.

We have made progress. I don't think anybody, no matter how powerful, would dare or care to speak like that in today's America.

3.

While the subsistence farmer was doing his subsistence farming in the pioneer fashion, he probably did most of his own carpentry and blacksmith work. If he built a new cabin the neighbors would help him raise the frame, but the small work that one man could do with simple tools, a little at a time, he did. Or his son helped him. Or maybe his hired man. If, as the years passed, the farmer borrowed cheap money and had to pay it back in dear money, his independence might become a mockery. But mortgages and foreclosures came late in the history of the frontier.

In the market villages there were merchants and others who, as Thorstein Veblen loved to point out, might be parasitical on the farmer. But the village storekeepers, carpenters, blacksmiths, druggists and physicians had a sort of independence, too. Rural society, on the farms and in the small towns alike, had its tribal ways, but for a long time it was loosely organized.

4.

There is no denying that automation has cut into this perhaps deceptively simple life. In rural areas as well as in the swiftly growing cities things began to move on a more massive scale. Experts and specialists increased in number, even in the field of agriculture. There are buzzing factories where there was once farming land. The colleges and universities that once trained young persons for professional careers in medicine, the church, law, and several kinds of engineering, still do these things. They also offer a glittering and rigorous variety of courses in highly specialized technological fields. Corporations in search of technological aid not only compete for the spontaneous, free-wheeling graduates; they also offer scholarships and even endow professorial chairs. So does the Federal Government. In this period of swift transition the demand for highly focused specialists exceeds the supply.

Almost all these new jobs are labor-saving; they are for young people with high I. Q.'s and well-centered educations, who will take the places of many times their number of unskilled or semi-skilled workers—and even abolish the need for some highly-adept skilled workers.

The society of the future, it seems clear, will be compartmented, not by birth or wealth but by education and function. It may look something like this:

First, there will be the irrepressible executives, just as there are today, not necessarily full of wisdom but certainly full of drive and strategy. You can't run a society without these—you just have to watch them—and occasionally call them to order.

Second, there will be the technologists, who will also be needed to keep the wheels of society turning. (I don't say, the big wheels alone—I mean all the wheels, big and little.) These will have to see that the machines are properly designed, set up, supervised and continually improved. They will be so narrowly specialized that they may lose sight of the grand design that keeps humanity going forward.

Even today, the members of this group are like men in the armed services—moved around by orders from on high; assigned like sentinels to new positions, geographical and technical; perfectly secure economically but in danger of losing touch with the masses of their fellows. Indeed, they are the very opposite pole from Dan'l Boone, who packed up and sought new wilderness whenever things got so crowded that he could see the smoke from a neighbor's fire. They will be almost like interchangeable parts in a gasoline engine.

Third, there will be the men and women who actually preside over the machines—really skilled labor. They will not be quite so violently caught up in their jobs as are the technologists and inventors. They will shake the web of circumstance by going hunting and fishing, playing or watching games, perhaps, if television permits, even reading a book or learning a musical instrument.

Fourth, there will be various service occupations that do not require high skill but do demand experience and a sense of responsibility: postmen, policemen, firemen, bus drivers, airplane pilots, salesmen, and so on. Some might put physicians and nurses in this category: we'll certainly have to have more and more of them, better and better trained.

Fifth, there will be creative artists in various fields: artists, musicians, composers, writers, some researchers, and possibly philosophers. It is hard to classify these. It would be harder still to do without them.

Sixth, there is and always will be a residue of the unskilled, the incompetent, the inexperienced, and possibly the congenitally lazy. The sick in mind and body will have to be listed here—perhaps for cure, certainly for understanding and compassionate care.

5.

Such classifications are not rigid, they are merely convenient at the moment in a seething and changing world. The real test of our society is in the sixth or residual group, which is often a puzzle to itself and everybody else. The difficulty is that this rag-bag of humanity is not, like apples, potatoes or rabbits, a specific classification. It is simply what we have left after everybody else has been allotted a place. It may include the above normal as well as the below normal, the saint as well as the sinner, the genius as well as the moron.

I believe that for most normal people work is a pleasure, not a penance. But what kind of work? I am sure that such varying personalities as Saint Francis of Assissi, Galileo, Cellini, François Villon, Walt Tyler, Tom Paine, and other were all unfit for employment by anybody who needed steady and reliable help; but all worked hard enough, each in his separate way, to put humanity in his debt. They might remind us of the treasures of life wasted because of sick environments and mean necessities. We might find such men as these among the forlorn castaways in any period (if ever such a period comes again) of desperate hard times.

In the depths of the great depression of the early 1930's I went as an employed and working journalist to a public employment office in New York City, and sat with the others for a while, on the hard charity benches, as though I were

myself one of the unhappy applicants. The experience de-
pressed me, for I thought, but for the grace of God there
might I have been in sober earnest. My fellows on the
benches were almost all well-dressed. They looked subdued, like people in church thinking of their sins or drivers
waiting to plead guilty in a traffic court.

When I got inside the man in charge told me something
about them. Few were there because of serious discernible
faults of their own. Some had been well-paid executives.
There may have been some rebels and misfits, though I
didn't pick out any. There may have been a genius or two
and a fool or two. But some fools, I had noticed as I went
about the earth, had kept their jobs. There was no sensible
system of selection in operation.

In a better-organized society (such as we may have
today—or possibly we will have to wait until tomorrow)
these men and women would have been regarded as just
another undeveloped resource—an opportunity, not a problem. Unemployment is not a real puzzle for a community
that is run as intelligently as we can now operate a nuclear-
driven power plant.

6.

I have been talking about several topics but in each case I
have been relating them to the true individualism or lack of
individualism in our society. This is natural, it seems to me,
because a pure and unselfish individualism is one of the
most beautiful expressions of the human spirit. Its growth
can be traced (with many setbacks) through all known
history: its major planting in Palestine, its flowering in
Greece, its repression in Rome, its recurrence in Western

Europe after the Dark Ages, its fierce outbreak in revolutionary France, its slow and sometimes distorted growth in Britain and the United States. We cling to this pure dream with passion, even when it is imperfectly fulfilled. A century after the Gettysburg Oration we still intend, though we know it still evades us, a new birth of freedom.

The "democratic" nations of the Western world are setting the pattern of the future, and it is primarily scientific and technological and only secondarily political. This culture is spreading as the culture of the Bronze Age once did, for the same reasons, though on a vaster scale: it produces better results with less work. This is a force that cannot be dammed off, even by the mystical systems of the Orient.

The future is in the hands of the communities that can produce the most—and these are, I think, the communities that consist most nearly of free persons. Man may rise to his feet and straighten his aching back. He may still be in exile from Eden but the curse of Adam has been lifted from his shoulders.

Little by little, if he so wills it, the world around, the burden of dull and unhappy jobs will diminish. Such changes may take a generation or two to effect, but they are in any visible future rising out of present industrial tendencies.

Mankind has conquered or is conquering all other living beings, including the microorganisms. He has only one enemy left—himself.

Recessional

SOMETIMES I THINK we are going to make it and sometimes I am in doubt. The tangible arguments are all in our favor. It is the intangible considerations that bother me. Have we carried along in our swift development too many traits and qualities that were good when we lived in trees or caves but now do more harm than good?

We can do almost anything we like with the earth we live on. Are the things we like to do the sort of things that will make us merry and prosperous in the long years to come? Say, a thousand years. There is no use in being a prophet if you can't look at least that far ahead. For one thing, if you go in for good long forecasts you don't get found out so soon.

I am optimist enough to believe that mankind, having come through so much, will not be easily exterminated. Still, a cockroach might think this, too, and be just as right. We might both be wrong. Some astronomers say that the sun may wind up operations in about three billion years. But I think we had better wait and see, and in the meantime do the best we can with what we have.

But we have to answer the question that the Speaker of the infinite Houses of Heaven may ask: for what purpose does the human race arise? This is a query never yet satisfactorily answered. Action and reaction, common interests and mutual hostility—such has been our long, sad, dramatic, sometimes glorious history. But now our problems are no longer tribal; they are worldwide, and cannot be solved at all if the peoples of the earth do not achieve a common tolerance and understanding.

Let us not be sentimental about the brotherhood of man. It is a brotherhood of rights, privileges, and mutual respect, not an invitation to the whole of earth's inhabitants to drop in for tea or cocktails next Wednesday at four. We ought to love our neighbor or the stranger within our gates as much as we can, which is often a good deal; but for us to agree with all his curious ways and notions, or he with ours, would reduce us all to silent dullness. And in the long course of time, if the ceremonial killings called war were entirely ruled out, we might really come to love one another in a calm sort of way.

The history of two World Wars indicates that even the most arrogant propagandists can't make us deeply love a people or a nation; they can, however, induce us to hate or not to hate them. A ditty in that wonderful musical show *South Pacific* makes this catchingly clear: "You've got to be taught," it says, "to hate." It is easy enough to feel superior to people different from ourselves, but we have to attend classes and do our homework if we are required to hate them.

2.

Sometimes I suspect we are growing more civilized. I have noticed during a fairly long lifetime that the American public's enthusiasm for war has steadily diminished; it takes a lot of prodding now to make most of us eager for more shooting, stabbing, or bombing, even though we stay at home and look at television or read the newspapers while young men do the actual slaughtering—and dying.

This may be, of course, because the old type of fighting is not remunerative any more, costs fantastically, settles little or nothing, and disgusts those who have to participate intimately in it. If it is a big war, the soldier no longer marches gaily off to it, with the bands playing and pretty girls admiring him; he stays home, and his grandparents, wife, and children are likely to be in as much danger as he himself is. If it is a little war, as in Vietnam, it is just dirtier and more vindictive than war used to be—and women and children do get killed. I can think up just as good arguments for restoring slavery as there are for having any kind of war today—except, I suppose, in sheer self-defense.

War is played out. It never was much fun, except for the sports-loving gentry, and now it is no fun at all. Conflict, religious, economic and political, will long persist, but it will gradually dawn upon even the dullest brass hat and the most envenomed orator that these cannot be disposed of by the methods of the Chicago slaughterhouses.

Please observe that I am not predicting an increase in man's goodness. What we have to hope for is an increase in his worldwide common sense. In war's grim department store there is nothing we can buy, from now on, but our own death and deep damnation. The kindlier virtues will flourish if they are also the most prudent ones.

I would rather entrust final statesmanlike decisions to the kind of gathering I once saw in session in Rome; in an unmitigated awe I heard and beheld, not generals, admirals, or politicians (none of whom abash a former newspaperman), not princes, potentates, and the other riffraff of power—but a gathering, in brief, of Nobel prize winners. Plato, who wasn't present, would have been pleased, I think.

3.

So here we all are, Nobel prize winners, ordinary citizens trying to be prophets—and bums. We are all still struggling to master the supreme science of getting along peaceably one with another. Now we come before the great court of destiny, a whole generation of us, more than three billion in number, with a plea in avoidance, setting forth why we should not be evicted from the lands, privileges, and emoluments we now hold. Is it our fault that we have met the conditions forced upon us by Nature for our survival? If we had been a soft, easy-going lot we might not be here now. There is, in fact, some evidence that one or more humanoid races disappeared, simply because they were too good-natured and willing to oblige. We do not have to fight sabre-toothed tigers any more or deal with glacial periods. But the old firm qualities—too many of them, it often seems—still persist in us. Stir us up a little, especially in groups and mobs, and we become ferocious: a prime military virtue but not of much use in today's civil life.

We find it hard to settle down. We fight with one another, not always in war. A few of the superfluous pugnacious traits may have been bred out of us—but let us not count on this.

We remain a part of nature (spelled with a small "n"); a man sitting in an airplane traveling two thousand miles an hour or creating a brand new desert by plowing up the grass on the Great Plains, or composing a symphony is just as much a natural phenomenon as a trout in the water or a swallow on the wing; the impulse to act in this way was put into him long ago—though in man's case the means to do many of the things he is doing were made available only yesterday. We used to throw coconuts; now we have H-bombs. The principle is the same.

But we have learned to do tricks never before performed in front of any audience. And this is our danger and our glory. We have arrogated to ourselves the God-like right to decide which of our fellow creatures shall surive, which shall serve us, and which shall perish. The great depths of the sea may still contain many living creatures whom we have never met, but this social error will in time be rectified.

We plow, we pave, we pour sewage into the once clear waters of upland lakes (take a long, slow look at Lake Tahoe, for example), we cover the earth with our structures, we use up the buried resources, such as coal, oil, iron, copper, aluminum, phosphates, and strange metals known only to specialists. We store great waters to irrigate and to manufacture power—flooding out the natural life on plains and hillsides to do it. The deep wildernesses—so-called not because they were truly wild but because no men were there—hardly exist any more.

We have made some islands radioactive and have contaminated the atmosphere by our lethal bombs. We have cluttered the atmosphere with enough hardware to set up a chain of stores.

The worst thing we do is to kill without thought, destroying forms of life we cannot replace. (I don't doubt future scientists, tinkering with the *genes* in their laboratories, will be able to create new monsters—but who wants monsters?) But has anybody seen a heath hen recently? Nobody will, for there are none. Or a swarm of passenger pigeons? We are trying now to save the whooping crane but we probably started too late. We preserve some rare animals, reptiles, and birds in zoos, but this is an afterthought. Wild life is on reprieve (as though we ourselves weren't as wild as any of the others) in a man-dominated world.

We can't go back and undo the possibly mistaken things we have done. We have to go on and do what we can. And what is that?

4.

Some features of creation, indeed, we have left almost untouched. There are wide-open spaces in Antarctica. Many of us have seen parts of Labrador and Newfoundland from the air, and these are not noticeably cluttered with human artifacts. Nor is Northern Alaska, or the Sahara Desert. We will attend to this, however, if anything valuable to us, such as a uranium deposit, turns up there.

We are sitting pretty, as our remote ancestors would have put it, in whatever tongues they spoke. We are no longer much hampered by heat, cold, or sterility in the soil.

Whatever we want we go and take, and we are able to arrange at least the interior climate of any place in the world. (General management of the climate will probably come later; give us time.) We have come a vast distance since the first of us, naked and shivering, came down onto the ground and out in the open, and looked furtively at every bush and rock to make sure no anthropoid-eating creature was lurking behind it, ready to pounce.

Our survival looks as though Something or Somebody planned it that way. Why? If our mental equipment had so much survival value why didn't other creatures go in for it, too? Did we have a sort of celestial patent on it? Or did the Grand Designer experiment with other animals and find us just too charming to throw away? The elephant works for man, or did when I last heard from India. Why don't we work for the elephant, whose trunk is almost as ingeniously contrived as our hands? And what is there in the human race, at least in its primitive dawn-forms, that would inspire favoritism? Read some election returns, at home and abroad. What is there in them to declare the wisdom of our species?

We ourselves may be the dawn-men, and our descendents, if we allow them to be born, may be infinitely superior, far wiser, archangel types with feathered wings. But here we are, by accident or design, too far advanced to be wiped out by anything short of a full-fledged Fourth-of-July cataclysm; here we are, seeing everything from a human point of view, treating the earth as though it were a mighty machine and we the appointed engineers; here we are, penetrating into mystery with our five senses. But we do not and cannot know the entire universe. There may be depths beyond depths, circles within circles, that we can never perceive, because our five senses, however reinforced with the most ingenious instruments, are not enough. Do these suspicions alarm the terrified reader? I hope so—they terrify me.

There are many things to be uneasy about. I have mentioned some of the more familiar ones in the preceding pages. We can choke ourselves with too much population; we can slaughter each other in war at a magnificent rate; we may perish from diseases not yet invented.

We can kill ourselves in spirit if not in body by giving up the effort to make freedom live and flourish; we can wreck such civilization as we have by living in hate and fear with our neighbors; we will surely die if we of the perhaps over-ripe Occidental countries do not relieve the misery and the jealousy of the retarded nations and races.

A perfect human society is impossible. If we had it to fit anybody's definition we would perish of tedium. We shall not, I believe, be saved by any miracle of invention, nor by any sort of planned society. Our communities will grow more comfortable, but never comfortable enough; free from the more insolent forms of tyranny, but never wholly free from the often irrational pressures of society. We shall always find it hard to keep our boots off other people's toes, our elbows out of other people's ribs. But we will be better supplied with what we think we need, and better informed, and our manners, even under stress, are likely to improve.

I wonder if we can retain the true spirit of adventure, the mingling of fear and exultation that comes with mountain climbing and new discoveries by land and sea. We will always need the salt of danger that makes palatable even a diet of unrestricted abundance. The space walkers already enjoy this, but we cannot afford to send many young men strolling around on nothing or hibernating on the inclement moon.

5.

If I had a utopia it would be a negative one. Individuals living in it would continue to do many things they ought not to do. The young would persist in shocking their parents, and the other way around. People who drank too much alcohol in the evening would continue to have headaches the next day. Politicians (and many others) would still regard persons who ventured to differ with them as ignorant, dishonest, or malicious. The whole world, and every community in it, would still be full of jealousies, rivalries, and turmoil. Though we would have better ways to prevent local and general bloodshed. Psychiatry would take care of many of these troubles, and ways would be found to keep the psychiatrists from becoming too uppity.

It is not utopian to feel sure that our machinery will be improved—I doubt that this will make anybody the least bit happier. We may be able to go from New York to Calcutta in three hours. Why? Disease of various kinds, including cancer and circulatory ailments, will be conquered or subdued—including the disease of traffic deaths. There will not be so much meaningless routine. We will live longer and be more comfortable and energetic while alive. Government, political and economic, will be more efficient than it is today, but the struggle between the individual and the organization will continue. If we are able to restrict the numbers of the human race we may be able to improve its quality. But I don't know how to do this—not this afternoon. I hope it won't be attempted in the laboratory.

I trust that the men and women of the future will be curious enough to keep on hunting for the ultimate truth. We seem to be the only animal that ever took a deep interest in the subject. We will never find this ultimate—there is too much of it and not time enough—but it is fun trying. If we ever did find this secret I suppose the whole universe would break up like a punctured soap bubble. But I am not worried.

If we do not survive I imagine some other creatures will. Except for the sudden explosion of the sun (turning it, as the briefly delighted astronomers would say, into a "nova") the earth will no doubt continue indefinitely to nourish life. And as the twenty-second verse of the eighth chapter of the Book of Genesis promises, "Seedtime and harvest, and summer and winter, and day and night, shall not cease."

I believe our great show, with humanity as the leading character, still has quite a time to run. This is partly because I cannot imagine a purposeless universe. It may be difficult to believe in a majestic Meaning, somewhere up in the sky, but a vast Meaninglessness is even harder to accept. Can a beetle happen? Can a trout? Can a red-winged blackbird? Can a man? Can Shakespeare, Dante, Beethoven's Ninth Symphony, and Abraham Lincoln?

Nothing is less explainable than what the astronomers see with their telescopes and measure or assay with their spectroscopes and their electronic instruments. It's there, however.

The cultural history of our race, if a human being is competent to say so, is astounding: the development of food stuffs such as wheat, Indian corn, the potato, rice, millet; the taming of useful domestic animals; the mastery of metal-working; the growing control of natural forces; the endless curiosity about everything, including ourselves; the growing mass of knowledge; the outward gazing, if not the actual journeying, into infinity; the instinct toward freedom, which often sleeps for generations, then revives; the majestic procession of the saints and martyrs who loved their fellowmen and suffered for them: can these achievements, from which we all benefit because we are human, be no more than the casting of the celestial dice, of no meaning and of no avail?

Perhaps. Perhaps not. Life in some form, beauty, grace, intelligence, sense of humor, aspiration toward things unseen and unknown—these may be spread like points of light throughout the vast abysses of Being; we may be writing on a celestial slate that can be studied for a moment (and a moment is all we ever had) and then, with a wisp of damp cloth, wiped out.

Perhaps. I don't think so. I think we mean something in the universe, and will go on. But of one stern fact I am quite sure: the fostering female we have called Mother Nature (not to be confused with some inconceivably vaster deity) has finished with us and moved on—perhaps to another planet in another system—if there is such. Our future will be what we make it.

We've been weaned.